YOUR CAREER IN
TEACHING

arco's
CAREER GUIDANCE SERIES

YOUR CAREER IN
TEACHING

Neil Hartbarger

ARCO PUBLISHING, Inc.
219 Park Avenue South, New York, N.Y. 10003

Published by Arco Publishing, Inc.
219 Park Avenue South, New York, N.Y. 10003

Library of Congress Cataloging in Publication Data

Hartbarger, Neil.
  Your career in teaching.

  (Arco's career guidance series)
  Bibliography
  Includes index.
  1. Teaching—Vocational guidance.   I. Title.
LB1775.H347   371.1'0023   79–14287
ISBN 0-668-04741-0
ISBN 0-668-04752-6 pbk.

Printed in the United States of America

CONTENTS

FOREWORD

A career in teaching? In a time of declining enrollment and closing schools, such a choice seems unlikely. But one of the best features of Neil Hartbarger's book is its candor. The author does not paint a rosy picture of expanding opportunities and easy work. Instead, he tries to describe in clear terms the reality of teaching, the importance of teaching, and the personal satisfactions of the work.

Harbarger does not seek to entice people into a profession by describing only the ideal schools, best supervisors, and most appreciative communities. The author assumes that many new teachers will work on tough assignments in struggling schools. In fact, in his attempt to show the realities of schoolteaching, he leaves out many of the bright spots. Not all administrators are as narrow in focus as he suggests, for example. And many school principals are educational leaders, not just disciplinarians. Similarly, there are far more lively and interesting schools than one might think.

The real reason for choosing teaching is the personal satisfaction of doing important human service. Neil Hartbarger recognizes this. He says in effect that if you want to *work with people,* if you want a *profession that serves deep human needs,* if you want to have a *lasting impact,* choose teaching. It's not easy, but it is important in the deep ways that satisfying human careers should be.

Francis Roberts

Francis Roberts
Distinguished Specialist in
Education and Social Policy
Bank Street College of Education

INTRODUCTION

Since you have gotten as far as reading the introduction, you must at least be a little interested in teaching. But, your thoughts about it are probably rather general. You know what teachers do because you have attended school. Teaching may appeal to you because it seems idealistic; you would be helping people to learn about the world and about themselves, and, ideally, you would be changing their lives for the better. Maybe you love children and want to work with them; or, perhaps you are academically inclined and want to stimulate and challenge others' minds.

You're looking at this book to find out if teaching is really what you want to do with your life. Of course, nobody can make that decision but you. However, this book will give you an impartial, realistic look at what a teacher's life is like, the education required, the special challenges you might not have been aware of, the employment opportunities, and alternative areas of employment that include some teaching responsibilities.

Teaching is an honorable profession. It can be argued that it is the first profession; nobody could become a doctor or a lawyer, an architect or a social worker, a brickmason or a chemical engineer without being taught by someone else. Of course, some people claim to be self-taught, but they taught themselves by seeking information from others either directly or indirectly.

Teachers help people learn to live in the world by communicating facts, ideas, theories, methods of drawing conclusions, and ways of gaining information. In addition to all of this, teachers serve an important social function. They help students to develop *social personalities*. Under the watchful eye of a teacher, children learn to work side by side. A sensitive and thoughtful teacher can have a considerable, positive effect on a child who is beginning to have trouble at home, with his peers, or in school.

It is the teacher's responsibility to give students the skills and perspective necessary for complete development as individuals and as citizens. Some teachers do not achieve this admittedly lofty goal. It is an unfortunate fact that some schools have become mere processing centers, endeavoring to pass children through school with as little disruption of the system as possible. It's also unfortunate that some teachers belatedly find themselves in the wrong line of work or become tired and jaded by year after year of teaching the same material. Neither situation is good for children, who are required by law to attend school for a certain number of years. A child who is caught in a compulsory process that seems to care very little for his or her needs and wishes can learn frustration very early.

There are good teachers and bad teachers. This should be no surprise; teachers are like everyone else. However, it is especially important for those who wish to become teachers to be suited for it.

Some teachers believe that they have low social status, that people don't think highly of the teaching profession. They complain of receiving comments such as, "So when are you gonna quit teaching and get a real job?" "What do you do all day besides wipe little kids' noses?" "Those who can, do; those who cannot, teach." That last bit of nastiness is especially misguided. Many teachers who are very capable in their chosen fields have decided to teach in order to share their knowledge and skills with others.

It is apparent that these comments have grown out of a genuine hostility toward teachers. But why should anyone think ill of a profession as positive and idealistic as teaching? It may be that those people who speak badly of teachers are insecure in their own work. They *know* that what a teacher does is important, but they are not so sure that their own work is. By downgrading teaching, they make themselves feel better. There may be other factors as well. They may have had unpleasant experiences in school; or, they may resent teachers for seeming smarter than the rest of us.

The point is that teaching is a very sensitive area. Teachers are in the public eye, and they may find themselves in the middle of a controversy if someone does not like the way they are carrying out their responsibilities.

In spite of the drawbacks, teaching affords many rewards. One of the greatest is the chance to watch people grow, and, sometimes, to assist in that growth. Many teachers mention the pleasure of seeing a student understand a concept for the first time or come up with an original idea.

There are other rewards as well. As a teacher, you belong to a group of educational professionals, and the company of these highly skilled and intelligent people is often quite stimulating.

In the rest of this book you will discover more of the rewards of teaching, many of them spoken of by teachers themselves.

YOUR CAREER IN
TEACHING

1 WHERE ARE THE JOBS?

It's unfortunate to have to begin with bad news, but it is unavoidable. There aren't very many public school teaching positions available. The following quotes all indicate how widespread this is:

> "The Pattonville Board of Education voted 4-1
> Monday night to cut 35 of the district's 560
> teaching positions for the next school year."
>
> The *St. Louis Post-Dispatch,* February 15, 1978.

> "Paul English said school officials 'can be much
> more selective' about hiring teachers because there
> are about 10 applicants for every one available
> teaching slot."
>
> The Oklahoma City *Daily Oklahoman,* February 23, 1978.

> "Due to an oversupply of teachers, it is possible
> that there will be a moratorium on new teacher-
> training programs in Idaho colleges."
>
> The (Boise) *Idaho Statesman,* December 10, 1977.

> "For the first time in the history of the Cedar
> Rapids Community School District, certified staff
> —mainly teachers—may be laid off next fall."
>
> The *Cedar Rapids* (Iowa) *Gazette,* February 2, 1978.

> "The National Education Association reported
> that there were 94,050 job openings for teachers in
> 1976, and 185,850 graduates of education
> programs."
>
> The *Charlotte* (North Carolina) *Observer,* January 31, 1978.

Those figures indicate that there are almost two job-seekers for each job—and that does not include former teachers who want to rejoin the profession, who swell the total to 302,850. That might not sound like very good odds, but you must

1

remember that you will only be looking for one job. If you had been looking for a teaching position in 1976, and had the proper credentials, you would have had 94,050 chances for a job as a teacher.

Of course, many teaching jobs are filled very quickly. Some school districts have waiting lists of highly qualified people who would love to teach there if a job opened up. But there are many other areas where teaching jobs go begging. This condition is also confirmed by newspaper articles.

> "Despite a national oversupply of teachers in most subject areas,...Baltimore has had trouble finding teachers, particularly in math and science. ...The city will need to hire at least 150 teachers by September."

> The *Baltimore Sun,* February 4, 1978.

> "There is a shortage of teachers in Community School Board 22, in the Flatbush section of Brooklyn."

> The *New York Daily News,* February 3, 1978.

> "There is currently such a teacher shortage in some school districts that teachers who have no more than provisional teaching certificates are being hired."

> The *Los Angeles Times,* February 12, 1978.

What Is the Problem?

What is the reason for this situation? Why is the teacher job market in such a mess? Why are there ten applicants for each teaching position in Oklahoma City and not enough math teachers in Baltimore?

In many cases, the situation boils down to urban problems. Many teachers don't want to work in cities where there has been a lot of urban decay. Consequently, there is a shortage of teachers in those areas.

Whether you are an English teacher or a learning skills specialist, it is relatively difficult to get a teaching job in the affluent suburbs. You will have a somewhat easier time if you choose to work in a rural area. City schools, especially in cities where urban blight has set in, are the easiest labor markets of all. A good gauge of a city's problems is its age. Older cities, like the East Coast, Great Lakes, and California cities, have had the longest time to decay, and thus to develop problems.

Of course, there are some other factors. Depending on the teacher's area of specialization, s/he may be more or less in demand. For example, a school board may have a long list of applications from qualified English majors, who, in addition to competing with each other, must contend with the fact that most schools already have enough English teachers. On the other hand, there aren't enough teachers trained in math and the sciences. Aspiring teachers who majored in these areas stand a much better chance of finding jobs. In fact, there are some specialties in which the job situation compares favorably with employment in private industry. These areas include the various vocational specialties, remedial reading, speech therapy, and, particularly, special education. It must be noted, though, that specialized training is needed for each of these, and this sets them apart from other areas of teaching.

As you study to become a teacher, you will find a special area of interest. Your interest may be young children, so you will tend toward becoming an elementary school teacher or some other elementary school specialist. You may find that you are most interested in math or science; thus, you will specialize in teaching that. You should always keep in mind, though, that the specialty you choose will have a direct bearing on the ease or difficulty of your post-college job search.

Many people who are interested in the humanities (i.e., literature, languages, the arts, philosophy, religion, communications) tend toward teaching. The result is that there are more candidates for teaching positions in those general areas than there are in math and the sciences.

There are also more candidates for teaching positions in areas that require the least training; or, put another way, the more training you have, the more job opportunities will be open to you.

The conclusion that can be drawn is that it is harder to get a job teaching high school English than it is to get a math-teaching job. Prospects are better for a teacher trained in remedial reading, or someone who can teach a vocational subject such as automotive repair. The best prospects are for those trained in special education, that is, education for those who are physically, emotionally, or mentally handicapped, or who are unusually intelligent. Although there are other reasons for the great demand for special-education teachers, a major factor is that the rigorous training required for special-education certification tends to limit the number of qualified applicants for a position.

The upshot of all of this is that if you choose your area of specialization carefully and do not limit yourself to teaching in a particular location or type of school, you can increase your *employability* tremendously.

Scarcity of Jobs

Why are there relatively few teaching positions available?

Although there are a number of reasons, the primary cause is declining school enrollment. The "baby boom" is over, and the number of school-aged children is declining in virtually every state. This situation has placed school boards in a very difficult position. There are fewer schoolchildren, so schools are not being used to full capacity. It is not economically sensible to operate eight schools in a district when six schools could accommodate the number of children adequately and more efficiently. To keep costs in line with enrollment, some schools must be closed. The result of this is displaced personnel.

Generally speaking, there have been no instances of teachers being laid off. However, when a teacher retires, or leaves for some other reason, the position simply is not filled. Consequently, the normal turnover that used to provide jobs for most people who wanted to become teachers has started to disappear. The in-and-out flow of teachers from year to year has become, to some extent, a one-way flow. This has cut down markedly on the job openings for new teachers.

Another factor has compounded the problem. For many years, the administrators of teachers' colleges and teacher-education programs at universities blithely ignored the predictions of declining school enrollments. They continued to graduate teachers, but paid little or no attention to finding jobs for them. Their point of view was that they were supposed to train teachers; that placement and job counseling were others' responsibilities. They trained some excellent teachers, but they were not *needed*.

This point of view fits in well with the American ideal that *more is better*. But nowadays that idea is being questioned. Teachers' colleges have belatedly acknowledged that students require assistance even after they graduate. Most of these institutions now provide practical, useful career counseling to their students, and even to prospective students. This should ease part of the overproduction problem, because it will help to ensure that only those who really want to become teachers go through a teacher-training program.

In addition to the bumper crop of teachers and the light crop of children, other factors have led to the shrinking number of jobs for teachers. An important one is economics. Inflation has pushed costs up, especially municipal budgets. Towns are looking for ways to cut costs, and part of the cuts are in the personnel budgets for schools. This, coupled with a new reluctance on the part of taxpayers to put up more money to support their schools, has tightened things considerably.

As teachers have begun to form unions, the school boards' attitudes have hardened toward salary and benefit requests. A new militancy—almost an adversary relationship—has developed, and there have been a number of teachers' strikes.

A Look Ahead

The U.S. Bureau of the Census has been keeping an eye on school populations, and they observe that the elementary school population peaked in 1970–71. Their prediction is that it will reach a low point in 1978, nearly 12 percent lower than in 1970. The good news, however, is that this population is expected to increase again very slowly through 1985. Although this will allow educators to recover somewhat from the great drop of 1970–1978, it will not cause a marked increase in the number of teaching positions. Excluding other considerations, conditions should stabilize and the size of teaching staffs should level off. The unofficial hiring freeze in many public school districts may be lifted, allowing some retiring and otherwise departing teachers to be replaced. The result will be a much healthier atmosphere in which to work and teach.

In addition, enrollment in teaching programs can be expected to drop, at least somewhat. This will ease the degree of competition you may face as a job candidate. Word is getting around that it's tough to get a job as a teacher, and this will tend to steer the fainthearted or less committed to another line of work. Many state-supported teacher-training programs are going to be scrutinized by legislators and state boards of education. Funds for some programs may be cut, thus allowing admission of fewer students, and some may be eliminated entirely. This, again, will act to cut the competition. Of course, it will also make it harder for you to get into a teacher-training program. Ideally, only the most qualified and dedicated students will complete the training to become teachers.

Funds for schools will continue to be tight, and may get tighter. There is a new mood of conservatism abroad in the land, and taxpayers aren't happy about rising tax bills. One result of this has been the taxpayer revolts in many parts of the country. The most famous of these went under the banner of "Proposition 13" in California in 1978. There, voters slashed the state budget through a public referendum. In effect, they said, "We're not going to pay as much in taxes as we have been paying"; and they left it up to the state's bureaucrats to decide where to make the cuts.

Education is already a big part of most states' budgets. Because of federal cutbacks in education funding and federal court rulings that shift the burden of paying for schools from local school districts to state governments, education will become an even bigger part of states' budgets. States will be caught between increased responsibility for school funding and the voters' demands for limited spending. A likely result is that there will be less money for schools.

Changes in styles of teaching will also have an effect on the future teacher job market, though whether these changes will have an expanding or a shrinking effect is not yet clear. "Team teaching" is currently a popular idea. As the name implies, instead of there being one teacher per classroom, there would be two, or more, teachers per classroom. The situation may be handled in any of a variety of ways; one teacher may be a specialist in certain subject areas or may deal with students' specific questions or problems, or both teachers (or more) may work more or less equally on the same material with all of the students. The benefit of team teaching is its flexibility. There are many possibilities, and the teachers can try out a variety of combinations to see what works best to deal with specific learning problems. Whether this will provide more teaching jobs depends on how it is used. If more teachers per classroom simply means an increase in the number of students per classroom, the number of teaching positions won't increase very much. If, on the other hand, more teachers teach the same number of students per classroom, there will obviously be a greater number of teaching positions available at that school. It must be noted, though, that only the most affluent school districts will have the money to be so experimental.

Another innovation, the teacher's aide, may serve to cut school costs. Aides don't have the education of fully accredited teachers, but neither do they have the responsibilities. The aide's role is mainly to lift some of the clerical, red-tape duties from the shoulders of the regular teachers, who will, thus, have more time to teach. This allows schools to spread their teachers farther and, because aides are paid less, to save money in the process. The long-term effects of this innovation are not clear yet. It probably will not serve to increase opportunities for teachers, except in schools where the savings are put toward teachers' salaries. It will, however, increase job opportunities for teacher's aides.

Special Opportunities

It's a familiar rule in the career counseling field that crisis situations create new jobs. If someone has a problem that he can neither avoid nor cope with by himself, he has to hire someone to take care of it. If you are looking for a job market's "weak spot," this is it. If you can find a problem and qualify yourself to solve it, you can get paid to do the job.

Two crises in education today require immediate responses. The first is a requirement by the federal government that certain, previously ignored groups, notably women and the handicapped, be given equal educational opportunities. Women's sports programs have been broadened and more money has been provided for women's teams. In many cases, this has caused major shakeups in physical education departments. The prize-winning football team that the alumni love costs a tremendous amount of money, and all of that money is spent on a game that, generally speaking, only men play. Now, some sort of a fair distribution is required.

Although money is slowly beginning to trickle into women's sports programs, the people to administer those expanded programs are still needed. Voila! Jobs! The opportunities for both women and men exist at all educational levels.

In the past, handicapped people were either educated in private schools, at tremendous cost to their families, or not educated at all. There were organizations that helped provide funding, and some money was available from the government, but it wasn't enough to guarantee every handicapped child the opportunity to get an education.

The federal government now maintains that every handicapped individual has the right to receive an education. In many cases, local school districts have become responsible for providing this education, either within regular classrooms or through special facilities. People with the proper training, usually in special education, have had to be hired. Thus, more job opportunities have been created.

The second crisis is concerned with *Why Johnny Can't Read.*

The average scores of recent Scholastic Aptitude Tests indicate that children are not learning as much or as well as they used to. Parents are screaming about the poor education their children are getting, college admissions officers are screaming about unprepared freshmen flunking out of their first semester's classes, and personnel officers are screaming about unqualified job applicants. Above all the voices is a call for people who are trained to teach students to know how to read, write, do simple math, and, above all, how to study. In this general area, positions are available in such fields as remedial reading, basic math, study skills, and some related areas, such as counseling. Having the educational background and the ability to teach basic skills *well* is an advantage in getting any teaching job.

The Silver Lining

It is clear that although there aren't as many jobs in teaching as there are in many other lines of work, there are some encouraging signs for those who are really committed to becoming teachers: job prospects are improving in some areas and the

School librarians may help younger children select books to read, or they may help older pupils find reference materials and other source material.

trend is now shifting, if only slightly, from the teacher-oversupply/student-decline situation. This was indicated most strongly in a recent article in *U.S. News & World Report.* The story quoted source after source to the effect that more and more teaching jobs are going begging, teachers are leaving their careers earlier to go into other lines of work, and fewer and fewer new teachers are entering the market. Frederick R. Cyphert, Dean of Ohio State University's College of Education, was quoted as saying that the school's placement office found jobs for 98 percent of the college's 1978 graduates.

You, too, *can* get a job as a teacher. The following chapters should help you decide whether you want to be a teacher and, if so, in which field.

2 CREDENTIALS

There was a time when willingness was the only credential a person needed in order to teach; knowledge of the subject was secondary. Later, the town fathers became more selective, requiring that a teacher know something about what was to be taught. Still, there were no standards for choosing a teacher.

Of course, all of that has changed. Educational requirements are quite strict throughout the nation. A bachelor's degree and some additional credits in education is a national standard, and a master's degree is becoming more important as the world grows more complex and more advanced credentials are required.

Minimum Education

Generally speaking, there are two educational paths to becoming a teacher. The most common way has been to take an undergraduate program in education. This might be through a teachers' college or through the college of education at a university. In either case, the college will offer several routes, depending on your educational specialty (i.e., elementary education, kindergarten-through-twelfth-grade, secondary education, vocational education, etc.). Whatever your specific program, the basic education program courses include educational theory, child and adolescent psychology, measurement and interpretation, teaching methods, and classroom teaching experience. In several cases, you will also take courses in your area of specialization (chemistry, for example, if you plan to be a chemistry teacher).

This list of courses may seem a little imposing, especially if you have not yet begun your college career. You shouldn't let that put you off, though. These courses are spread out over four school years. In addition, undergraduate education programs do not have a reputation for being particularly difficult; there are many required courses with a great deal of work, but they are not impossibly difficult.

Once you have graduated, usually with a B.A. in education, you can apply for certification from the state board of education. In some states you may have quite a long wait. In New York, for example, there is currently a delay of several months between application and certification. You can usually find out this time lag from your college's career counseling center. It's a good idea to line up some temporary work in the meantime. One possibility that also offers teaching experience is that of a teacher's aide, or *paraprofessional.*

The other major path to teaching certification begins when you graduate from college with a bachelor's degree in whatever field you have chosen. To qualify for certification, you must take a certain number of graduate-level courses in education, many of which are the same courses taken by undergraduate education majors (education theory, methods, measurement, and, of course, classroom experience).

Many people go through college not really knowing what they would like to do once they graduate. Quite a few of them end up with degrees in English literature, sociology, or psychology, but without a clear idea of what to do with their degrees. These particular disciplines are well suited to the training of teachers. Literature teaches an understanding and love of words, the stock-in-trade of most teachers. Sociology describes the behavior of people in groups, which is what most teachers deal with in their daily work. Psychology examines the behavior of people as individuals, which is important because teachers must be aware that students have individual needs, strengths, and problems.

One teacher, a graduate in psychology, speaks with an understandably prejudiced point of view.

"At the risk of insulting a lot of people, I have to say that teacher ed is *the* worst college education you can get if you want to teach. You can actually manage to get through a teacher ed program without taking a single child or adolescent psych course. I think that's shameful.

"I never had a single undergraduate education credit. Now I have the minimum ed credits to teach here. Most of those classes were workshops. But I think I'm much better equipped with my psychology bachelor's than somebody who went through teacher training.

"I strongly believe that even up through high school, you're still teaching the child, not the subject."

Of course, there are equally staunch defenders of teachers'-college education, and these institutions have produced a tremendous number of skilled and committed teachers over the years.

The Master's Degree

Education is keeping up with other professions in its use of more highly educated people. This means that in many states you will need a master's degree in order to teach. And the way the world is going, it will be more the rule than the exception in the future. This is part of the logical progression of education. In early times, you needed no formal education beyond the ability to *do* whatever it was you were supposed to teach. If you could read and write, you could teach others to read and write. However, the world has grown more sophisticated; thus, more education is required to teach.

You don't have to have a bachelor's degree in education to get into a master's program in education. This is encouraging to people who have liberal arts degrees. If they would like to teach, they can, in most instances, get the credits in a graduate program without having to go back for undergraduate courses. In fact, a B.A. or B.S. in a non-education field can be useful if you're planning to teach in a particular area, such as math or chemistry, or to become involved in an educational specialty, such as counseling or school media.

A B.A. in education is especially helpful if you are planning to specialize in elementary or early childhood education. Many undergraduate education programs are geared specifically to train teachers of young children.

Master's programs are quite a bit more rigorous than bachelor's programs. Most graduate schools require that you maintain a 3.0 grade point average (a B average); otherwise you will be put on academic probation and possibly dropped from the program. And you will have to work hard to get those A's and B's. You will probably be required to complete a research project and a thesis or project report as part of your degree requirements. You may even face comprehensive examinations.

As it becomes harder to qualify for a teaching position, there will be fewer new teachers. It's a strange twist on the old "good news, bad news" joke: the good news is that fewer people will be competing for each job; the bad news is that it's getting harder to get the degree that will allow you to compete.

Special Qualifications

Certain teaching specialties require specialized education. Included among these are special education, counseling, vocational education, and reading and speech therapy. Although each of these will be discussed in depth in its own chapter, the following briefly indicates the additional or unusual education that is needed.

Special education teachers are qualified to teach children who have unusual educational needs. These children may be physically handicapped, may have emotional problems, may have some form of mental retardation or learning disability, or may be unusually intelligent. All of these children are considered to have special needs, and their teachers need special training. In most states, a master's degree in special education is required to qualify for this job.

School counselors, also called guidance counselors, have a range of duties. Most school counselors are employed in

Soon these student teachers will be on the other side of the desk—in a classroom of their own.

secondary schools and may do anything from writing college recommendations for graduating seniors to talking to students who are having trouble in school or at home. Counselors usually help students plan the following year's curriculum at the end of the school year. A B.A. in counseling and guidance is the minimum qualification for counselor certification, and most states require a master's degree. In addition, a valid teacher's certificate and two years' teaching experience is generally required. Some states will allow a year of professional internship under a licensed counselor to be applied against part of the teaching requirement.

Trade and vocational teachers have the most unusual requirements for certification. Because they teach occupational skills, such as auto mechanics, they are required to have work experience in addition to a certain number of college-level education courses. Because of the way the requirements are structured, it is possible for certified professional teachers not to have graduated from high school.

Reading teachers and speech therapists deal with children who have learning problems or speech handicaps. The requirements for this position may differ from one state to another; in some cases, experience as a reading teacher may be one of the major qualifications.

Continuing Requirements

Although many states give temporary certification to applicants who have a bachelor's degree, most require additional education for a permanent or renewable certificate. This usually entails having earned a master's degree, although some states will accept 30 semester-hours of course credit as the equivalent. This option can be a great opportunity. Even though an advanced degree is eventually required, if you can get a job with only a B.A., you have the opportunity to work, gain experience, and, possibly, get some tuition assistance as you work toward a master's degree. Although it takes longer to get the degree this way, it is usually less taxing economically.

Who's in Charge Here?

The state or territorial government certifies all of its public school teachers, usually through a board of education. The criteria used in different jurisdictions vary, and the best way to find out specific regulations is by writing to the board of education in the state capital. (You should be able to find the address in the library.)

A summary of teacher certification requirements is provided in the appendix. The information is current as of 1977, but because changes may have occurred since then, it is a good idea to write for specific information.

3 THE TEACHING LIFE

The introduction to this book briefly touched on the factors that motivate people to teach. Money is definitely *not* one of those factors. A recent study indicates that teachers earn 20 to 30 percent less than federal employees having equivalent education and responsibilities, and 30 to 40 percent less than their counterparts in private industry. Nationwide, the highest average for teachers during the 1977–1978 school year was $18,375.

The accompanying table should give you some idea of salaries in the various regions of the United States. Remember that you have to consider the local cost of living when making comparisons among regions. For example, because the cost of living is nearly 20 percent higher in the Mideast than it is in the South, the higher salaries are partially offset by the higher cost of living. (The information was collected and prepared by Educational Research Service. ERS publishes an excellent series of reports, available in some school professional libraries and a few public libraries.)

*Average Salaries 1977-78

Region	Classroom Teachers	Librarians	Counselors
New England	13,597	14,450	15,943
Mideast	15,066	15,552	18,570
Southeast	11,726	12,304	13,658
Great Lakes	14,211	14,838	16,922
Plains	12,746	13,446	15,553
Southwest	12,655	13,867	15,388
Rocky Mtns.	13,028	14,141	15,784
Far West	16,516	17,916	19,485
Nationwide	13,941	14,739	16,641

*©Educational Research Service, Inc.

This chart shows that teachers are paid the least of the three professions listed (these three were chosen because they provide the most educational services to a school's students) and that the average salaries in the Mideast and Far West regions are the highest, while the salaries in the Southeast, Southwest, and Plains states are the lowest.

Whatever the differences, teachers still aren't paid very much when one considers that they are highly trained professionals, many of whom hold advanced degrees. This unfortunate fact of the teaching life is something that anyone interested in becoming a teacher must face.

The Rewards

Many people do go on to become teachers; thus, there must be other incentives besides money. The reasons are probably as diverse as there are numbers of teachers.

"I started teaching eleven years ago. I was in my first year of law school. The only problem was that I was number 24 in the draft lottery. So I became 'instant teacher'—I found out they were giving a special draft deferment for guys who would teach in ghetto schools. In those days they'd hire you to teach if you were breathing. I took twelve hours of classes to get my New York State temporary certificate, and started teaching full time the next fall. My school's in the South Bronx.

"I planned to teach until the war ended or the law changed. But the more I did it, the better I liked it. I like watching the kids grow up. The best part was my first three years. I taught first grade, then the same group of kids for second and third grades. I've also taught fourth and fifth. I really like the kids, and I think I'm good at what I do. So, instead of quitting, I stuck with it. And here I am today, a thirty-three-year-old elementary school teacher."

Another teacher had a similar story.

"I can't say I ever intended to teach. I had a B.A. in English and I couldn't get a job. This was about five years ago, and you could still get teaching jobs in public school, so I immediately went back to school and got an M.Ed. in reading. I had very little trouble getting a job in the Boston schools teaching reading.

"I only taught reading for a year. Then the law changed in Massachusetts and all reading teachers were grouped under special education. My assignment was to set up a resource room for learning-disabled kids in high school. I'd had exactly one course in learning disabilities, but I guess at that time that made me qualified.

"It was excellent experience. Like I said, I had never intended to teach, and this was the perfect job for a teacher with that kind of orientation. My major responsibility is helping kids cope with crises. The kids who are my responsibility are all having trouble in school or at home. I have to help them any way I can to make some kind of success at school. So it isn't really teaching. But it is, too."

Mona, on the other hand, didn't just fall into teaching.

"I always knew I was going to be a teacher. Always. I never even considered doing anything else. I think my coming from a Hispanic background had something to do with it, because I knew that people in minority groups couldn't go very far in life without a good education. Education was always very important to my family. They took my grades and school work very seriously. That's very rare nowadays. You never see kids getting the kind of support from home that my friends and I did when I was growing up. So I feel like my job is even more important, because I have to provide what the families aren't.

"It gets me in trouble sometimes with my kids because I come on a little strong. But I'd rather do that than leave them to live the life so many others live. It kills me to see twelve-year-old kids hanging out on the street. Once they reach that point, their chances are pretty much gone unless some kind of miracle happens. They'll be hanging out on the same corner with the same nothing in their pockets and in their heads when they're fifty.

"It's a sort of power trip being a teacher, 'cause sometimes you feel like maybe you can do something to keep that from happening. I'd never do anything but teach. They're never gonna retire me. I'll die a teacher."

Family background seems to have a lot to do with a person's decision to become a teacher. Take Tony, for example.

"I come from a long line of teachers. Both my parents, my grandfather, my uncle; they were all some kind of teacher—college, high school, kindergarten. My grandfather was a divinity school professor, and I guess he was a major reason I wanted to teach. Like a lot of little kids, I sort of fixated on him, tagged along, listened to every word whether I understood what he was saying or not. He and my mother and father used to have these long intellectual conversations about philosophy and religion, and I'd sit very quietly and listen. I was in love with the words, I think, because I don't remember anything they said, just the sound of the words they used.

"There was a silent assumption around my home that there was nothing more noble or important than teaching. It would have been surprising if I'd become anything else with that kind of environment."

Some people who want to teach have a hard time realizing their ambitions. Peggy works in a bank because, with her education, she can't find a teaching job.

"I have an A.A.S., associate in applied science, in early childhood education. I went to a little, two-year, Catholic college for my degree.

"The only job I'm qualified to do is to be an assistant teacher in nursery school through second grade. There aren't too many jobs around, and for every opening there are fifteen or twenty people lined up. I'm competing against people with master's degrees and teaching experience for the same job. They'd be crazy to hire me, with all those degrees to choose from.

"When my husband gets his promotion and things are a little easier financially, we're both going back to school—him part time, me full time. There's no way I'm going to work in a bank all my life. I want to be a teacher.

"I want to teach first grade. I love children. That's the main reason. When I was student-teaching in college I worked in a first-grade class and I loved it. It's so nice to watch them learn to read. For most of them it's all new, and they're really learning something.

"I want to do something with children. When I was young, I babysat for little kids. I was also a mother's helper. I really enjoyed it."

Each of these people had different reasons and motivations for becoming teachers. Some chose teaching out of necessity: to avoid the draft or to get a job with a minimum of difficulty. These motivations are no less laudable than the simple idealism or love of children expressed by the others, because they brought effective and compassionate teachers into the educational system. And it is the outcome that is most important. Either the love of teaching and students was there from the beginning, or it grew as a result of teaching experiences.

Some of these teachers have left the profession, and they are missed. Their reasons for leaving are the other side of the coin, the disadvantages and problems faced by teachers.

The Problems

One major problem is the low salary. In all likelihood, this situation won't change in the future. The primary reason is that the money just is not there to pay teachers what they should be receiving. Schools are expensive, teachers' salaries are the largest part of school budgets, and taxpayers are not willing to pay much more than they now pay to support their schools. This condition places a limit on teachers' salaries, a limit there does not seem to be much hope of removing.

Another related problem is that once you are a teacher, there is nowhere to go. Teachers do not receive promotions because there is no position to which to be promoted. The only position to which a teacher may be promoted is that of department chairperson. This person chairs meetings, acts as official liaison between the school administration and the department's teachers, sets certain work rules, and determines some of the department's educational goals. The chairperson is still a teacher and has classroom responsibilities. Generally speaking, a chairperson's salary is significantly higher than that of a regular teacher. Unfortunately, the position is a reasonable goal for very few teachers. There are few of these jobs compared to the number of teachers. Those who are promoted to the post are most often teachers who have seniority. In addition, as in any public-service job, politics plays an important role.

Teachers may also move up into such administrative positions as assistant principals, principals, or, perhaps, school superintendents. However, this isn't an easy step to take. Additional college-level education is required (usually graduate courses in school administration). This education can be expensive, and admission to graduate programs is rather limited. Approximately one quarter of the nation's school districts reimburse teachers for college expenses, but many teachers report that the amount of the reimbursement is not nearly equal to the cost. As was mentioned earlier, teachers are not highly paid; thus, trying to get the extra education to qualify for a more advanced position can put a financial strain on a teacher who has a family to support.

For the majority of teachers, *advancement* means moving up through the pay scale set by the board of education. The scale is usually based on two criteria: amount of education and years on the job. This simply means that a teacher who has a master's degree and thirty extra credits earns more than one who has a bachelor's degree, and that a teacher who has been working in the school district for six years earns more money than one who has only been there for two years. This can be a source of frustration to those who see teaching as a challenging profession. They may be highly motivated and interested in working hard and carving out a place for themselves, but the structure of the system encourages those who seek additional education and who stay with the job for a long time. The go-getters are not rewarded; and the emphasis on being reliable and supporting the administration tends to leave the mavericks out in the cold.

Another common complaint among teachers is that of having little social status.

Steve A. knows how it feels.

"The people I grew up with are into other things that I see as more successful and of higher status. Things like running their own businesses, working in hotshot law offices, that kind of thing. I know it's not really true. What they do is maybe even less important than what I do, if you can measure things like that. But that's the way people think about teachers. When you say you're a teacher, they start talking down to you; or even worse, they just don't include you in the conversation, like you couldn't possibly understand their conversation because it's about something out in the *Real World.* You pick some of that up. You can't help it. And it makes you a little insecure."

His sentiments are echoed by Jan, a teacher in an affluent suburban school system in the Northeast.

"When you say you're a teacher, the conversation ends. I think it's offensive. I was at a party a few weeks ago, and this orthodontist was holding forth on how he relates to adolescents. An orthodontist, for heaven's sake! Here I am with a degree in adolescent and child psychology and years of high school teaching experience, and these people are asking an orthodontist for advice on how to relate to their kids. They think they know exactly what you do, that you couldn't possibly have anything interesting and worthwhile to say. I'm a professional, damn it!''

Teachers have to fight against a slightly negative public image of their profession; you might call it the *Old Maid Schoolteacher* image. Historically, teachers just were not taken seriously. Teaching was a job for unmarried ladies who could do nothing else and to whom society gave no other role. No other job was considered proper for a *nice* woman. Since women's abilities were not considered significant or important, the teaching profession got the same reputation. It was obviously a slander on both the women and the profession, but it has stuck in one form or another. The great strides that have been made in teacher education and accreditation of schools, not to mention increased status for women, have only begun to make a dent in public attitudes.

The *feminine* image that teaching has acquired also poses a problem for men who are interested in entering the profession. The problem is especially acute in elementary schools, where teaching males are still something of a novelty. It might cause some discomfort to men who are susceptible to being typed as somewhat less than totally masculine. However, the situation does have one advantage for men. Because it's somewhat unusual for a man to apply for a teaching job (even in these enlightened days), it gives him a certain advantage in hiring. Schools are particularly sensitive to charges of sex bias in hiring because of recent Federal government rules and court rulings. Thus schools look favorably on an opportunity to balance out their faculty.

Long-time teachers say they detect a change in public opinion regarding the value of an education. The last generation grew up believing that a good education was the key that unlocked the door to the good life, both materially and intellectually. But that faith isn't as strong today. Many teachers complain that students are not getting the kind of educational support they should get from their families.

"It wasn't like this when I was growing up," one young teacher argues. "All of my friends had to study—their parents made sure of it. We all were made to know that school was very important and that we were to 'apply ourselves' and do well.

"Today that's not the way it is at all. On school nights, my students do their homework in front of the TV—if they do it at all—and then go out 'till all hours with their friends. 'School nights'—that phrase used to have some kind of almost sacred significance. 'You know it's a school night,' our parents would say. 'You can't go out, and that's final.' Sometimes I think my students' parents couldn't care less. And then they blame us because the students' achievement test scores aren't high enough. We aren't miracle workers."

The one exception to prevalent educational attitudes described above is a trade school education. Parents take that kind of schooling very seriously. We will go into detail on vocational teaching in a later chapter.

Another complaint voiced by many teachers is that they are required to fill out so much paperwork that it interferes with their teaching. This is especially true in the case of special education teachers. Recent federal rules require teachers to fill out a complicated document for all students with proven special educational needs. On the form, the teacher must spell out each student's abilities, special requirements and problems, and the teacher's educational goal for the student. This form is called by a couple of names, the most descriptive of which is "Individual Education Prescription." It runs about 14 pages when completed, and it takes several hours to fill out.

Of course, this is the extreme case. But there is one document that is the bane of every hard-working teacher's life—the lesson plan. Virtually all school districts require a teacher to prepare a written plan of what will be taught in a day or a week and give the written copy to the school administration. The theory behind this is that it guides the teacher in planning how to teach a certain concept or subject, and it gives the school administration some idea of how well a teacher is covering the state-required curriculum. Most teachers don't like it. "It's another example of the ridiculous bureaucracy we have to deal with," Walter C. says. "There's absolutely no correlation between good teaching and lesson plans. But it is a handy way to rate teachers. The first year I taught, I used to get into heated discussions with the assistant principal about lesson plans. It came down to 'If you want to teach here, you file your lesson plans.' I handed them in—under protest—and never heard anything more about it. Now I just file and forget them. I pay absolutely no attention to them after they're written."

It seems to be a mark of pride with many teachers that they pay so little attention to the lesson plan requirement. One woman admitted that they might be useful for a first-year teacher with no experience. "But an experienced teacher doesn't need that kind of guideline. I usually fill out mine a month in advance so I don't have to bother with them as much."

The Valley of the Shadow

Here, we should point out an unpleasant aspect of teaching these days. It shouldn't put you off from considering teaching as a career, because the world needs good teachers, and you might become one. But you should know about it nevertheless.

The problem, in a nutshell, is that school can be a dangerous place. Many teachers have to face hostility and sometimes violence from their students, students' parents, and strangers who come onto the school grounds. It is a problem that only now is beginning to be discussed. This is information you may not get from your school counselor or from a college of education.

Many urban and suburban schools have security personnel who make regular rounds to combat school crime.

In December of 1978, *The New York Times Magazine* reported on the problem. John Kotsakis, a representative of the Chicago Teachers Union, had this to say: "It would be difficult for a school of education to tell its students that 30 percent of the time they won't be teaching, they'll be policing. We can't expect education schools to say to students, 'You're going to work in schools that are depressing and run-down.' "

The magazine article went on to say:

> "Alfred M. Bloch, a Los Angeles psychiatrist who has studied and treated several hundred battered teachers, found that they unconsciously expect students to see them as loving, protective, wise parent figures. The typical assaulted teacher, Dr. Bloch says, is extremely idealistic and passive, traits which keep him from understanding, much less handling, violence directed toward him."

This last idea is most important. Teachers are *unprepared* for what they may have to face in actual on-the-job conditions. Teachers' unions are now taking a more active role in helping their members cope with the violence directed against them. But a more viable overall solution to the problem is to prepare teachers before they have to use their wits (or their feet) to escape a dangerous situation.

Today's teacher, especially in an urban school, must be at least one part social worker and one part police officer to teach effectively.

Teacher Burnout

Teacher "burnout" is sometimes the ultimate result of all the problems listed above. The stresses and frustrations of the job are just too much for some people. They get tired, depressed, bored, and beleaguered. They may develop physical symptoms, ranging from dandruff to ulcers and heart attacks.

The result is that many teachers leave the profession. In the 15 years from 1961 to 1976, the proportion of teachers with 20 years' experience dropped by 50 percent. So the problem of teacher burnout has been an evolving one. By all accounts, though, it is at its worst in today's urban schools. Teachers see it as a culmination of students who don't care about school, an administrative structure that is unresponsive to teacher needs, decrepit school buildings, tightening education budgets, a worsening of their individual economic situations, and the depressing atmosphere of being around other teachers and administrators who are also burning out.

There's an informal consensus among teachers interviewed for this book that the useful lifetime of a teacher is a maximum of 10 years, and probably less. "After that it's downhill all the way," one eight-year veteran said.

School and union officials are trying to attack the teacher burnout problem from various angles. Many of the urban teachers' unions provide counseling for their members. Some school administrators rotate teachers among different grades from year to year to keep the challenges fresh. Some teachers try to approach their jobs in new or different ways, such as working part-time or sharing one job with another teacher—both ways of giving teachers more leisure time and a new perspective on their jobs. Colleges and universities are offering courses to help teachers understand the forces currently acting on them. But the most viable solution seems to be to prepare teaching school students for the realities of the jobs they will go into when they graduate. Teaching students are increasingly reluctant to take their student-teaching experience in the tough inner-city schools. But they have to face the fact that that is where most teaching jobs will be found in the future. Those jobs have to be filled, and the people who fill them should be prepared to do a good job for their students and for themselves.

A Teacher's Day

Now that you have been "terrified" by visions of giant students armed to the teeth to attack poor, defenseless, burned-out teachers, let us bring the discussion back into perspective. Let's follow a real teacher through a normal day—one without great calamities or problems beyond the day-to-day responsibilities of teaching.

We met Walter a few pages back. He was the teacher who was so indignant about having to turn in his lesson plans to the school office. As a matter of fact, today is the day he drops off his week's plans. He spent about two hours last night preparing the neatly typed sheaf of papers. He's learned from other more experienced teachers to keep copies of lesson plans from year to year. That way he has a relatively simple time of preparing the same plan with minor modifications the next year.

His school day starts at 7:40. He strolls into the teachers' lounge and grabs a cup of coffee. Coffee-drinking is almost an addiction among teachers, because coffee breaks are about the only time they get to socialize with people their own age. He has ten minutes to exchange pleasantries with the other teachers, drink his coffee, and tie his tie before going to his fourth-grade classroom down the hall. He has found that even fourth-graders respect him more if he dresses carefully.

At 7:49, Walter starts toward his classroom. On the way, he drops off the lesson plans with the receptionist in the principal's office. He's running a little late—he usually tries to get to his room before the kids get there. The place is a madhouse, with nine-year-olds running around, hanging up their coats, dumping each other's books on the floor, and generally making a large noise. They quiet down (with a few scattered giggles) when he walks to the front of the room. He waits a few extra minutes to give them a chance to finish their business. He claims it's the key to his keeping their attention as well as he does—he gives them a chance to be playful kids for a few minutes so they'll be more attentive students when it's time for work.

Walter has settled into a comfortable and effective routine for getting his kids through the fourth grade as painlessly as possible. He has also set up a series of rules for himself:

1) Always be scrupulously fair to the kids.

2) Make the class rules very clear at the outset and stick by them.

3) Absolutely no playing favorites.

4) Remember that they are children, not small adults.

If there's a problem in class, Walter believes he is more likely to be causing it than the children.

Although Walter has not been able to live by his rules at every moment, overall they have served him well. His pupils seem particularly relaxed and reasonably attentive.

Walter spends a few more minutes shuffling papers and talking quietly to a few children, because he knows that a series of announcements will shortly come over the public address system. While he listens to the announcements with half an ear, he silently takes attendance and reviews the previous day's work so he knows where and how to start.

"Okay, everybody in your seats," orders Walter. "George, are you gonna start the day making trouble? Now give Willie his shoe." George complies. "Who's going home for lunch today? Got your notes? Okay, pass them up to my desk." Walter thinks that this is the slowest part of the day. The rest flies by.

The first subject the class reviews is arithmetic homework. They spend about 20 uneventful minutes on it. The kids are already dividing up into those who like numbers and those who do not. By 8:20 they are ready for a change of pace. Walter's favorite pace changer is what he calls "reading the newspaper." He pulls out a newspaper and reads an article; then he asks the children to explain it. He figures there are at least three benefits to this exercise (in addition to the fact that he gets to read the paper):

1) The kids sharpen their language skills by analyzing what he reads to them and restating it in their own words.

2) They learn a little about the news.

3) They learn to carry on a conversation.

In his first year of teaching, Walter was amazed to find that some of his students had no idea of how to interact socially with an adult or another child.

Walter keeps track of the time constantly, because when he's having a good time teaching he tends to forget that his attention span is longer than that of a normal nine-year-old. Only a few bells ring during the day to tell teachers what period it is, so the teachers must make sure they do not run overlong on one subject and have to cut time off another to fit all the subjects into the school day.

Soon it's time for the children to go outside for recess. Walter doesn't have playground duty this week, so he stays at his desk and fills out some forms from the state board of education. The board wants to know how many of his students have physical handicaps—hearing or sight impairment, speech difficulties, or mobility problems. He marks down one for Michael, who's been in a wheelchair since he could sit up. And Jennifer may have amblyopia—a vision disorder in which a child uses only one eye, even though both are functional. She's going to the eye doctor on Thursday. Walter had noticed that she seemed to have difficulty following moving objects (thrown balls, for example) with her eyes.

He looks for a "maybe" spot on the form. None. That's what he hates about these computer forms—it's impossible to qualify your answers. Just "yes" or "no."

At this point, his student teacher from the nearby state college of education rushes in, out of breath. She's a few minutes late for their conference. Today, they talk about some of the kids who are beginning to show behavior problems. Walter likes to set up a very conscious strategy for handling each child. For example, George likes to think of himself as sort of a hell-raiser (he was the one who had Willie's shoe). Walter's strategy is to pay as little attention to George's disruptions as possible. When Walter cannot ignore George's behavior—which happens relatively often—he handles it quietly and with a little humor. That way they stay friends and George doesn't get embarrassed. George is at heart a little shy, and embarrassment would probably be bad for him.

Maria, the student teacher, takes notes on their talk, first because it's complicated and she wants to remember what they say, and second because she's writing a college paper on the class's behavior problems. She'll stay in the classroom for the rest of the day, helping and observing. She comes to Walter's school for parts of three days a week and has classes in college the other two days, plus the early part of every morning. She will graduate in another year, and she plans to go right on and get her master's in special education.

Maria's advisor had explained to her that if she went looking for a job with only a bachelor's in elementary education, she could hope for a job only in either a very rural, poor area or in a ghetto school. Maria knows that children in these areas need good teachers even more than kids in a quiet suburban school. Still, she thinks it's best to qualify herself fully for what she wants to do. It's tough enough for holders of master's degrees to get hired.

The children come back inside, faces flushed from the cold. They say hello to Maria—"Ms. Querto"—and a couple of the girls hang around the desk to talk to her. They have attached themselves to her because she's female and young, and she has become a character in their romantic fantasies. Walter sends them back to their desks so he can get the class started on social studies. Maria takes a couple of kids to the "library" they have set up in the back of the room to work on their reading. She and Walter have already planned whom she will work with today. They made sure that her group consists of not just the slow readers—they want to prevent the class from being divided into the successful and the unsuccessful, especially by something as basic as reading.

Meanwhile, Walter has three kids up at the front of the class acting out the meeting between the Pilgrims and the Indians. The scene reminds him of an American cliché, like something out of a Norman Rockwell painting. But acting things out really seems to bring home to the kids exactly what happened and why.

Suddenly it's lunchtime. It seems as if only 15 minutes has passed since school started. Walter goes to the teachers' lounge. Today there's a lunchtime union meeting. One teacher has heard that the board of education is planning to cut down on the number of teachers' aides allotted to each school. That means teachers will have less free time, because the aides often take charge of the kids at lunch and on the playground. If the rumor is true, the teachers will have to do this from now on.

Emotions run high; the hiring of additional aides was one of the contract provisions the union won in the teachers' strike two years ago. The union still has not recovered from the strike penalties levied by the court. Three union leaders spent nine-and-a half days in jail, and the teachers lost two days' pay for every day they stayed out. It almost broke up the union, because it caused a lot of money problems, particularly for teachers with families. Walter had felt that the strike should have been cut short, but since then he has admitted that it was worth it. The school kept its assistant librarian (who was about to be "excessed"—a public school term for "fired"), the school board agreed to help fund a teachers' center that would provide counseling for teachers with emotional problems, and several aides were hired for each school in the district.

After much heated discussion, the teachers agree to get together casually with other union members to try to get the real story about the aides. Ironically, right at that moment, the school's four teacher aides are in the cafeteria, keeping track of the children. They don't even get to take part in the discussion.

After an unsatisfactory lunch (his stomach was upset by the cigarette smoke and loud voices), Walter stops by his department head's office. She's a 20-year veteran of this school system, and she's "seen it all," as she proudly says. He talks to her a little about the chance of another strike—she says it's impossible—and about a parent conference he has that afternoon. A new family has moved into the district, and their twin boys were assigned to his class. The kids have lived all over the world because their mother is an industrial engineer for an oil company. The boys have a kind of toughness, a shell, that he has been unable to break through. He wants to understand from the parents what forces are working on the children.

Walter has invited a college friend to talk to the class this afternoon. Nancy is an anthropologist, and she has spent the last three months on a research expedition in Brazil. She shows some color slides of the valley of the headwaters of the Orinoco River. Nancy is a good storyteller and keeps the kids spellbound for nearly an hour with stories about trapping monkeys, giant jungle insects, waterfalls, and exotic foods. Nancy promises to report back to the class on her further expeditions.

After Nancy leaves, Maria helps the entire class draft a thank-you letter. The kids suggest what the letter should say, and Maria writes each sentence on the board. When the letter is finished to everybody's satisfaction, one of the kids copies it down on a big sheet of paper, and everybody signs it. The page is decorated with pictures of monkeys and birds.

The school closing bell rings, and the kids are out the door in a flash. Annette and Willie stay behind for a few minutes to get extra help with arithmetic. When they leave, it's also time for Maria to go.

A few minutes later, the Caramanakises arrive to discuss their twins. Ivar Caramanakis is a quiet man with a slight accent —a naturalized U.S. citizen. His wife, Angela, is American. She speaks with a bit of a Midwestern twang. They seem intelligent, cosmopolitan people who are concerned about their children's happiness and success. They explain to Walter that Andy and Nathan have never had a chance to make close friends because they have moved around so much. Because of their isolation from other children, they have grown even more attached than is usual with twins. Angela says that she's not even sure if this is undesirable, because the boys would have experienced even worse disruptions from moving if they had had to leave behind a lot of friends.

Walter explains that the two boys seem intelligent and alert, but a little bored by their classroom experiences. He's afraid that because the twins have had so many experiences, what he talks about in class may be below their interest level. He asks details about the boys' background, so he can get a better idea of how to involve them in the class's activities.

The parent conference over, Walter heads home. This has been a short day; often, faculty meetings, parent conferences, or paperwork keep him at school until 5:00 or later. Today, he's getting home at 4:30. This is good because he wants to get some papers graded before he eats and goes over to the university. He's taking a three-hour graduate course in education program management so he can qualify for certification as an assistant principal. It will take him several more years to get all the extra course credits he needs, over and above his master's in education.

Marilyn, Walter's wife, isn't home yet. She is on a leave of absence from her research assistant job at a local electronics lab so she can go to graduate school full-time. Her company picks up 85 percent of her tuition costs, as long as she gets a *B* or better in each class. Walter jokes that if his school did that for him, he would be Dr. Walter Carr by now. He does get a tuition credit for his extra education, but the money is so little that it hardly makes a difference. So he is getting his advanced education slowly.

Walter tries to get to sleep by 11. After all, it is a school night.

Teachers' Unions

Teachers came relatively late into the ranks of organized labor. Although the history of teacher groups negotiating with management groups goes back several decades, the first major contract negotiated through collective bargaining was in 1962 in the New York City schools. Covered in the contract were salary scales, benefits (such as sick days and group health insurance), and some work rules.

During the 1960's teachers' union activity peaked. The union movement spread to cover a majority of the nation's school districts, and the unions negotiated advantageous contracts for their members that caused teacher income to increase at a rate faster than the cost of living—for the first time since the Depression. The nation's child population was booming, and teachers were in great demand. P.T.A.'s were active and often supported the teachers against the administration.

Teachers were in the front line in the war on ignorance and the war on poverty. They had respect—a new experience for most of them. Things were looking up.

Then the 1960's drew to a close. The Vietnam conflict ended, and the country slid into a postwar economic slump. Inflation increased, but income did not. People grew unwilling to pay more and more in school taxes. School boards began to win a few teacher union–board of education confrontations, then a few more. Since teachers are public employees, they are covered by "no strike" laws throughout the country. These laws were increasingly applied, and with greater effect. Union leaders went to jail until they called off their strikes, and members lost through salary penalties levied by the courts.

Both unions and school boards took tougher stands. But the teachers stood to lose more, and they often did. Certain benefits were dropped from older contracts, and salary demands were trimmed. Salary increases slipped below the inflation rate once again. Worst of all, teachers were getting laid off. The numbers of school-age children declined, and with fewer children, who needed all those teachers? The laying off of "unneeded" teachers came to be called "excessing"—a word that strikes terror in the heart of every "last hired" teacher in the land. It's the last hired who are first fired.

Let's backtrack a little on teachers' unions and explain exactly what they are and who belongs. A union is a group of individuals who share a common line of work—in this case teaching—and who elect representatives from their number to look after the welfare of the members, negotiate the terms of their employment with management, and call for unified action to enforce their demands. These actions can be strikes, sickouts (calling in sick and going to play tennis), "rulebook strikes" (going strictly by the employment rules and doing nothing extra), and a number of other tactics.

Some teachers do not belong to unions. One reason is that many teachers think of themselves as professionals who should not belong to a trade union. Doctors do not have collective bargaining organizations; why should teachers? They see the two ideas of professionalism and trade unionism as being mutually exclusive.

Other teachers do not want to pay union dues, which go to pay the organization's administrative costs and to add to the benefit and strike fund. However, in some school districts teachers pay union dues whether they belong to the union or not.

And some teachers do not see the benefit of a union. Why should they join an organization, give it a percentage of their salary, and then have to go out on a strike that they did not want and that will cost them a lot of money? And what good will it do in the long run?

Obviously there's a difference of opinion among teachers about the usefulness of the union. But it is a part of the teaching life for many, so you should know about it.

Fringe Benefits

To many people, teaching seems like the greatest job in the world. After all, how many jobs can you think of where you get three months' vacation from the first year on? The summer vacation cannot really be considered a true fringe benefit of teaching, though, because it is simply a function of the way the school year is set up. The real fringe benefits of teaching are things such as paid sick leave, a dental plan, retirement plans, Social Security contributions, hospital, surgical, liability, and life insurance, and sabbatical leave.

Teachers are well taken care of in the area of fringe benefits, compared to workers in other parts of the U.S. economy. For example, it is almost unheard of for a worker in other industries to get a sabbatical leave.

Summary of Selected Fringe Benefits for Teachers in Reporting School Systems, By Geographic Region, 1975–76*

				GEOGRAPHIC REGION					
	New England	Mid-east	South-east	Great Lakes	Plains	South-west	Rocky Mountains	Far West	Total All Regions
Percent With Vacation Leave	5.4	7.2	27.0	8.2	11.0	11.8	7.3	2.6	11.1
Mean Number Of Days Granted[a]	18	17	10	9	8	11	6	13	11
Sick Leave:									
Percent Granted Specified Number Of Days Per Year	93.2	96.7	98.5	97.4	96.3	100.0	97.6	98.0	97.4
Percent Granted Unlimited Accumulation Of Sick Leave	29.7	70.6	54.6	15.5	21.1	47.3	31.7	82.9	45.5
Other Leave Provisions:									
Percent With Emergency Or Personal Leave	90.5	94.8	90.8	90.5	89.9	86.0	92.7	96.7	91.6
Percent With Religious Leave	35.1	25.5	17.9	9.1	11.0	15.1	9.8	28.3	18.6
Percent With Sabbatical Leave	94.6	89.5	42.9	55.2	43.1	36.6	63.4	81.6	60.3
Percent With Severance Pay	39.2	49.0	29.1	48.7	25.7	23.7	29.3	2.0	32.2
Percent With Insurance Premium Paid By District:									
Group Hospitalization:									
Single—½ or more but not fully paid	63.5	17.0	15.3	21.6	15.6	21.5	14.6	14.5	21.2
—fully paid	32.4	81.0	50.5	75.4	69.7	17.2	75.6	69.1	63.2
Family—½ or more but not fully paid	68.9	26.1	13.8	29.3	33.0	9.7	9.8	23.7	26.3
—fully paid	27.0	69.3	13.8	47.0	20.2	...	26.8	42.8	35.0
Major Medical/Surgical:									
Single—½ or more but not fully paid	62.2	16.3	15.8	21.1	14.7	19.4	14.6	14.5	20.7
—fully paid	33.8	81.0	46.4	74.6	67.9	18.3	75.6	67.1	61.9
Family—½ or more but not fully paid	67.6	24.2	14.8	27.6	32.7	9.8	12.2	25.0	26.0
—fully paid	28.4	68.6	12.8	48.7	20.0	...	26.8	42.8	35.2

Dental Care:									
Single—½ or more	6.8	44.4	2.0	17.7	13.6	2.2	7.3	71.1	23.9
Family—½ or more	5.4	26.8	1.0	15.5	9.1	1.1	4.9	48.0	16.5
Vision Care:									
Single—½ or more	1.4	2.6	.5	1.3	.9	2.2	2.4	19.7	4.3
Family—½ or more	1.4	2.0	.5	1.3	.9	…	2.4	13.8	3.0
Group Life—½ or more	83.8	57.5	47.4	71.6	47.3	26.1	61.0	34.9	54.7
Professional Liability—½ or more	33.8	38.6	33.7	48.7	50.9	25.0	61.0	22.4	39.0
"Cafeteria Plan" For Group Insurance	…	…	1.0	…	1.8	…	…	13.2	2.3
Percent With Retirement Provisions:									
State Retirement System	100.0	100.0	99.5	100.0	100.0	100.0	100.0	100.0	100.0
Local Retirement System	…	1.3	5.6	4.3	3.6	…	2.4	1.3	2.9
Social Security	9.5	99.3	85.7	51.3	79.1	37.0	53.7	25.0	59.8
Percent With Tuition Reimbursement For College Credit	40.5	58.2	23.0	27.6	11.8	15.2	14.6	9.2	26.1
Percent With District Paying All Or Part Of Professional Organization Dues	5.4	2.6	1.0	.4	1.8	…	4.9	.7	1.5
Percent With Collective Negotiation Agreement For Teachers	89.2	91.5	33.2	86.6	70.9	31.5	73.2	60.5	66.8

States included in geographic regions. New England: CT, ME, MA, NH, RI, VT; Mideast: DE, DC, MD, NJ, NY, PA; Southeast: AL, AR, FL, GA, KY, LA, MS, NC, SC, TN, VA, WV; Great Lakes: IL, IN, MI, OH, WI; Plains: IA, KS, MN, MO, NB, ND, SD; Southwest: AZ, NM, OK, TX; Rocky Mountains: CO, ID, MT, UT, WY; Far West: AK, CA, HI, NV, OR, WA.

Fringe Benefits for Teachers, 1975-76. Reproduced with permission of Educational Research Service, Inc., Arlington, Virginia.

[a]For systems that specify a definite number of days. Systems that grant an unlimited number of days are excluded.

Tenure

There is one more important fact of the teaching life that you should be made aware of: tenure. In most schools, after the first three years of teaching you are granted tenure. This means that you cannot be fired unless you are proved incompetent or are convicted of a "morally reprehensible" act. The one other case in which a tenured teacher can be fired is when the job itself is eliminated. Thus if a school cuts down from four third-grade classes to three, one teaching post is eliminated. That allows the school to lay off one teacher, whether or not s/he has tenure. In this situation, a tenured teacher would be allowed to "bump" a nontenured teacher from another job (as long as s/he is qualified to teach in that position). If that is impossible (there are no nontenured teachers to bump), then the teacher with the least seniority gets bumped. This is the "last hired, first fired" syndrome.

This practice is uncommon in many other professions. The rationale for it is that teachers need to be able to teach, question, complain, and research without fear of reprisals from superiors. This goes under the general heading of "academic freedom." You cannot be fired because your principal does not like your teaching methods or the cut of your hair, or because the school administration has changed and the new principal wants to give your job to a friend.

Aside from protecting academic freedom, tenure also has unfortunate effects. Critics complain that it encourages mediocrity. If you can survive the first three years, they say, all you have to do is drift along for the remaining 20 or so years until retirement. The inducement of performing well to keep your job is removed, so you have no reason to put out much effort. Students suffer, and the overall quality of education decreases.

Both sides of the issue can marshall pages of statistics to support their positions. Your opinion will be formed by your experiences as a teacher. If you meet semi-incompetent teachers who come to class just so they can pick up their paychecks at the end of the month, you will have a low opinion of the tenure system. If you meet arbitrary, capricious administrators who would just as soon fire a teacher as brush their teeth in the morning, you may come to think tenure is necessary job protection. Whatever opinion you form, tenure will be a fact of your life as a teacher.

4 THE TEACHER TEST

By now, you should have a pretty good idea of the challenges and rewards of this ancient profession. It is time to look closely at yourself—at your personality, your intelligence, your emotional preparation—to see if the job is right for you and you are right for the job.

Look over the following questions. There are no right or wrong answers. The idea is to get you to think about yourself and your talents. Answer honestly and realistically.

Education (Your Own)

Do you have a love of learning? You don't have to love school—in fact, a healthy skepticism of school is an important attribute of a good teacher—but you should enjoy learning.

Are you good at academics? Do you study well and efficiently? You will need these skills to get through the four or five or more years of college necessary to get a teaching certificate. And it is unusual for a student who does not get good grades in high school to turn around suddenly and be a top student in college (even though it does happen). If your grades are good to excellent in your college classes, it gives you a tremendous competitive edge when you go out to get that first job. So be sure you can do the college work. You may be able to fool the admissions office, but you cannot fool yourself into getting A's on college finals.

Do you like the atmosphere of a school? If you cannot wait to get out of the door when class is over in the afternoon, you may feel the same way when you're a teacher. But then it will be too late to do anything about it.

Are you a good reader? Teachers spend a tremendous amount of time reading, even after they have graduated and gotten their jobs. If you're not good at absorbing information in this way, you'll have a significant problem as a teacher. You will not be as able to keep up with developments in your field as other members of your profession. Teachers can't afford to fall behind.

Personality

Do you feel you have a stable and well-balanced personality? There is nothing like a capricious or bad-tempered teacher to turn a classroom into an armed camp. You'll have to be able to take problems in your stride, and some of them may be major problems.

Do you feel good about yourself? People who don't often tend to manipulate others so they can make themselves feel better. They may belittle their students, or they may play favorites in order to feel that they have somebody on their side in class. It's bad enough when adults manipulate adults, but it's inexcusable to play power games with children. They do not have the defenses or perspective of adults to defend themselves.

Can you bounce back from disappointment? Teaching isn't always a bed of roses, and you'll have failures mixed in with your successes. It helps if you can develop relationships with your colleagues, so you can talk over your disappointments with someone who has probably experienced the same thing.

Can you relate well to other adults? Can you be honest about your emotions, and not feel you have to put up a front? If so, it will go a long way toward breaking through the feelings of isolation often experienced by young teachers. But many teachers have trouble here. They feel they have to keep up a front of cool professional competence, like a doctor's bedside manner. Perfection escapes all of us, and the ability to admit that can be a great release.

Can you take criticism from others? Teachers are a very critical lot, both of themselves and of each other. This criticism is usually meant to be helpful, but it can hurt. Can you look dispassionately at what your department head or a colleague says to you and take what is valuable?

Can you control your temper? Everybody has a temper. If you've never lost yours, you've simply never been pushed to the point of no return. Teaching is guaranteed to do this, so you should be able to control your emotions and return to an even keel quickly if the inevitable happens. Yelling is *not* a good way to control your class, for even if you frighten them into obedience, you have lost their respect. Children expect adults to behave predictably and fairly; if you don't, you lose some of your adult standing in their eyes.

Can you see the humor in a ridiculous situation? In other words, can you laugh when you might want to cry? Humor is an excellent way to defuse a difficult situation. On the other hand, you should never resort to ridiculing a student, whether in private or before the class. That is another entry in the list of inexcusables.

Can you laugh at yourself? The nature of children is to try to rebel against authority figures and, in the classroom, you're *it*. There is no authority figure so vulnerable to attack as one who is stiff and humorless. If you do something funny, your kids will laugh. If you don't laugh, too, they'll be laughing at you.

Do you have an idealistic urge to help other people? This sense of the importance of what you do can carry you through many low spots. It can give you the drive that will push you beyond being merely a teacher; you'll be someone who affects those around you for the better.

Can you relate well to children? All your education will be wasted if you cannot sit down with a young person and have a mutually satisfying conversation, on whatever level may be appropriate. By "conversation," we mean anything from a discussion about deepest feelings to the wordless interaction of play. You must feel that a child has something important to express. If that idea does not seem valid to you, you will probably have a hard time gaining the trust of your students.

Can you be open and accepting of other cultural values which may be different from yours? Public school has become the great mixing bowl of our country's many cultures. But experience has shown that today's school is not the "melting pot"

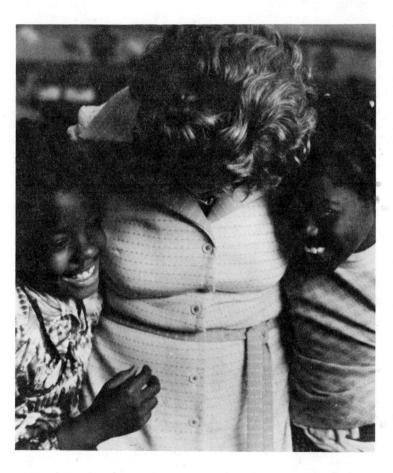

Above all, teachers must have a love of and respect for children.

expected by earlier generations. It is true that diverse groups have contact with one another in the schools. But this contact, the day-to-day exposure, has not resulted in a blurring of cultural differences, as social theorists of the late 19th century predicted. Our people have not become homogeneous; the differences still exist. So you will run into many people—students, parents, other teachers—who have different cultural or ethnic backgrounds from yours. These differences may breed mistrust if you allow them to. To make a success out of a teaching career in today's world, you need maturity, objectivity, and a tolerance for the ways of others.

Do you have the physical stamina to get through a school day? Teaching and interacting with children of whatever age for a full day is grueling. You will be on your feet most of the time. You will talk a lot of the time. You will be thinking all the time. If your body cannot stand the strain, you will not be a teacher for very long.

This does not mean that people with physical handicaps cannot be teachers. A handicap is not necessarily a constitutional weakness, and many teachers have learned to combine the needs of their profession with the requirements of their handicap.

Your Answers

You may have answered a lot of these questions with a firm "I don't know." Well, that's a good indication you have answered honestly. But even if you can't flatly answer the questions, you probably are leaning in one direction or another.

The purpose of this exercise is partially to get you thinking honestly about yourself and about what you want to do with your life. So get as much information on a possible career as you can. Look into some of the references listed at the end of the book. Write to the professional organizations to see if they have any career information to send you. Talk to teachers. See what they like about what they do, and what they don't like.

Talk to your counselor. S/he may have a wealth of information about a wide range of career possibilities. (Of course, some school counselors are so overloaded with responsibilities that the best they can do is point you in the right direction.) Talk to your parents. Tell them what you're interested in doing. Maybe they know some teachers who can give you sound background on the career search.

Talking to your friends about careers has both good and bad points. Good, because your friends are in the same boat as you, and they understand your need for information and advice. Bad, because they are no more experienced or knowledgeable than you are, generally speaking.

Go to the library. Tell the reference librarian that you want to find out about teaching as a career. S/he will probably be able to load you up with more pamphlets, books, and magazine articles than you really want.

Keep your eyes open for information. You need as much as you can get, because you are basing a very important decision on what you find out—your college and career plans.

Read the rest of this book. The following chapters will give you more specific information about the different types of teaching jobs, their requirements, where they're found, and if they have good job prospects.

5 PRE-ELEMENTARY TEACHER

What is a pre-elementary teacher? A pre-elementary teacher teaches children whose ages range from two to five years old, in nursery school and kindergarten. These are children who are not yet old enough to enter elementary school (grades one through six or eight).

Duties of a Pre-elementary Teacher

The responsibilities of kindergarten and nursery school teachers differ from those of other teachers in some significant ways. First, the teaching of academic subjects, like reading and arithmetic, is not a large part of their duties. The most crucial responsibility of a pre-elementary teacher is to assist the children in their psychological and social development.

This is not to say that children's proper development is *not* a concern of teachers in the higher grades. It is simply that the emphasis is different. In some early childhood schools, children under five get no formal training at all in reading or other academic subjects.

The teacher's day is also different. Usually, with children this age, the school day is much shorter than in elementary school—often only a half-day. So a teacher may have two separate classes of children: the morning class and the afternoon class. A great deal of class time may be taken up with play; the teacher acts in only a peripheral role and the children make up much of their own activities. But the teacher has a responsibility here to play that peripheral role well and with an understanding of the psychological level of the children s/he is working with. A certain amount of control and direction must be exercised to keep the class from resembling Pearl Harbor. Striking a careful balance between too much and too little control requires training and a great deal of understanding of a child's psychological processes.

The teacher also acts to expand the child's horizons by reading with the class, singing, leading a tremendous variety of games, and talking to the children on their own level. This ability to relate to a child on his/her own emotional and intellectual level is probably the most important ability of a teacher of very young children. It encompasses taking part in children's fantasy games as a participant, being able to throw off the adult notions of "proper" behavior and to bark like a dog if necessary, and generally to do nothing that imposes rules of behavior or thought processes that are too advanced for the level of the age group involved.

In short, you must let children be children. This is how they learn to be adults, *when the time comes.*

The teacher must also provide a good model of how an adult acts. Children need standards against which to compare their own behavior. They use adults as their standards and you, as their teacher, will be a prime candidate. You should be able to provide a standard that they can use without confusion. You should be able to act consistently and fairly and not pull any surprises on your kids.

You may experience a certain loneliness for others of your age near the end of the week, because the children you are teaching are of an age group that has very little understanding of you as an adult. In a strange way, you are both person and object to them at the same time. Person, in that they respond to you as someone with feelings and preferences; object, in that they respond to you as an obstacle to their games or as something to be played with. They have not yet finished grouping their environment into "things," "people," and "ideas," and they sometimes confuse one for the other. An example of this is the little boy who was playing with a car on the floor near a table. He pushed the car around and between the table legs, and was completely absorbed in his game. He decided to stand up; the table, obviously, did not get out of his way. When he bumped his head, he was very angry at the table for hurting him, calling it "stupid" and "mean." An adult might do the same thing, but the child was completely serious, and held a grudge against the table for the full length of his ten-minute attention span.

Another aspect of teaching this age group is that you must help them with many relatively simple things, such as going to the bathroom, washing hands, putting on coats, zipping zippers, and the ever-popular tying of shoes. After the first few weeks of teaching, you will find yourself dreaming of shoelaces at night.

A Normal Day

Nancy arrives at school a half-hour early on Mondays because it's her duty day. She must be there to keep an eye on the children that parents drop off at school on their way to work. The only people at school when she arrives are the custodial staff.

She drinks her morning cup of coffee with the head custodian, Mr. Walters, in his "office" in the storage room. The children trickle in and run to their classrooms to drop their coats in a heap under the coat hooks. She helps them find the hooks, then shoos them into her classroom so they're all in one place. Books and puzzles are scattered on low tables, and most of the kids busy themselves with these. She notices that, this early in the morning, they're pretty quiet.

She breaks up an incipient fight between Michael and Arthur over possession of a box of checkers by deciding that Michael should take the red checkers and Arthur should take the black ones. That quiets them for the moment. "Straight out of Child Psychology 219," Nancy thinks to herself. Later, she realizes that she wasn't so smart after all—there are checkers all over the school building.

The other teachers arrive and collect their classes. Soon, Nancy's left with her eleven four-year-olds.

She wants to take advantage of the comparative calm, so she calls her class over to the rug at one end of the room. The chil-

Teachers in pre-elementary classes must be aware of the special needs of very young children.

dren sit down in various approximations of a cross-legged position. They have established a routine; each child knows his or her spot on the rug. She sits down, too, with a stack of books that she plops in the middle of the group. "What book shall I read to you?" she asks. Several suggestions are made, and she makes the final choice.

After she reads for a few minutes, she shows them how to make chains out of strips of construction paper. A couple of the kids think this is insulting, "baby stuff." They learned all that last year in Mr. George's class. But the other children seem to find it interesting. Some do a little better than others, because eye-hand coordination develops at different rates in different children, and some are more advanced.

It's important that Nancy doesn't do anything for so long that the children become bored (which happens easily). On the other hand, she doesn't want to cut an activity short that they're enjoying. So the paper-chain-making goes on for nearly an hour before it degenerates into arguments over whose chain is whose and, worse still, whose chain is prettier.

Luckily, it's time to go outside and run around for a while. Nancy helps Joy get onto the high end of the seesaw, but Joy can't make her end go down because she's so much lighter than Davy, who's on the other end. So Nancy helps out a little by sitting on Joy's side of the center point. The two children think this is one of the funniest things they've ever seen, and they have a marvelous time making "Miss Marble" go up and down.

Time to go back inside. Nancy gives each child a small snack that they take to their chairs and eat. Then it's time for a rest. The children stretch out on the floor on their mats, and she puts some Bach on the record player, very quietly. "Music hath power to calm the savage breast," she tells herself. And, today at least, it seems to work. All that cold, fresh air has worn the children out. She sometimes thinks how much they resemble puppies. They play hard and romp for an hour or so, then rest for a few minutes, and then romp some more.

After the children nap for 15 minutes, Nancy turns on the TV set to watch "Sesame Street." The other teachers bring their classes into her room, because it's the largest classroom and because it has the TV set.

Nancy has seen this particular "Sesame Street" so many times she knows it practically by heart. She sits at the back of the classroom, talking to George, who teaches the class of three-year-olds. They have to keep their voices raised, because the noise level is high from the hilarity produced by 47 children all in one place. Both teachers keep their eyes on their classes, because it's easy for conflicts to erupt among the children in such close quarters.

When "Sesame Street" is over, it's time for the morning class to head for home. Each teacher helps the children on with coats and hats (for the second time this morning) and walks them to the door. The building is quickly empty, and the teachers gather for lunch in one of the classrooms. They look rather strange, all sitting at tables that are only 16 inches high. But none of them seems to notice.

Soon, when the afternoon classes arrive, they will repeat the same scene as in the morning.

Job Requirements

The job prerequisites for a pre-elementary teacher vary widely, depending on the state. Some states have set up very strict certification requirements that demand, at minimum, a bachelor's degree in early childhood education, and recognize the importance of a master's. Other states may have few or no requirements beyond a health department license to work in a school or daycare center.

The determining factor in the different requirements is whether or not the state has state-supported kindergarten and nursery school facilities. Those states which have pre-elementary public schools have the strictest requirements. States where early childhood schools are private or parochial often have the least stringent rules.

The final source for information on local teaching prerequisites is the state board of education. Its office is in the state capital, and you can get the address from the local board of education.

Personality Characteristics

Of course, the most necessary personality trait is a love of children. But that characteristic is not as simple as it sounds, because it must be coupled with an understanding of and compassion for their needs. It does not help to feel you would like to spend your days with cute little kids if you do not realize that they have some rather specialized needs.

A pre-elementary teacher should ideally have endless patience. If you recall, in Chapter 4 we mentioned that school-teaching would test your patience and your ability to control your temper. Very young children, especially, have the ability to try you, and it is crucial that you don't lose your temper. They can be strongly affected by what you say and do because they are so impressionable.

Besides being even-tempered and patient, you must be consistent. Children need your consistency so they know where they stand. It won't do to make a rule for your class and then allow a lot of exceptions. To the children, that means you weren't serious when you set the rule in the first place, and they won't take your other rules very seriously.

Related to this idea is firmness. You can't allow yourself to be manipulated by childish wiles into doing something you don't approve of. If the children know they can get away with things, they'll get a big kick out of doing it, but they won't feel very secure or taken care of in your class. It is very important that your students have a secure environment in your classroom. They need that first, because it helps them to grow into confident people, and second, because they will feel more comfortable in school for the rest of their school careers. Your class may be their first contact with school, and it will have a strong effect on their later feelings about school.

The last requirement is flexibility. Things will *never* go exactly as you had planned—in fact, they probably shouldn't. A really good teacher must have the imagination to take advantage of spontaneous occurrences in the classroom and use them to improve the children's experience and enjoyment. And you shouldn't let your rigidity keep you from enjoying the children. After all, it's one of the greatest pleasures of teaching.

Job Opportunities

The school population decrease hit the pre-elementary schools first, logically enough. Some school districts are now talking about cutting out kindergarten and prekindergarten entirely on the theory that these "grades" are not as necessary as the regular elementary grades, and elimination of very early schooling can cut costs significantly. So right now, it's a rather chancy employment field, at best.

There are many qualifiers to the above view, however. Some areas have many more young children than others, and those locales will have greater need of teachers for their young children. Young children often go along with young families. And young families often don't have a high standard of living. The conclusion you can draw from this is that you are more likely to find a pre-elementary teacher's job in a school district with a comparatively lower income level.

Public kindergartens and nursery schools are opening in areas that up to now haven't had them, notably the South. In many ways, the South is now going through the economic growth that the Northeast and Far West experienced in the 1950's and 1960's, and more money is becoming available to finance educational projects. So the job concentration may be greater there than elsewhere.

And you must remember that the numbers-watchers predict a slight growth trend in school populations through the 1980's. Just as the population decrease was first felt in the early schooling teaching areas, so will the first growth be felt there.

If this seems confusing, that's because it is. It is very difficult to come up with firm answers to the important question, "Will I be able to find a job?" There are many, many modifying factors. The only answer is to do your homework carefully and find out all you can that applies to your very own situation and goals.

6 ELEMENTARY TEACHER

Elementary school seems to have a nostalgic magic all its own, and some of the most memorable people from that period are our teachers.

The definition of "elementary school" varies from place to place. In some localities, it encompasses grades one through six, in others, grades one through eight, and in still others, kindergarten is included. Despite the variations, elementary school generally covers the first half to two-thirds of public school.

The Elementary Teacher's Duties

More than any other single responsibility, an elementary teacher must teach children *how* to learn within the confines of school, especially in the earlier grades. For many children, going to school is a difficult adjustment. It is not in their natures to be quietly attentive while a teacher stands before them and "instructs." And this adjustment process often takes more than the first year to accomplish. So, as their first responsibility, teachers have to make the transition to learning as smooth and easy as possible, both for the children's sake and for their own.

In the realm of subject matter, elementary school teachers lay the foundations for all later school learning. This goes well beyond the "three *R*'s" to include history and social studies, foreign languages, literature, and all the other subjects we learn throughout school.

The most basic skills children learn are the three *R*'s, however: reading, writing, and arithmetic. These skills are mastered, ideally, within the first four years of school. So teachers of these grades are responsible for assuring the academic success of their students in later grades. If kids do not get a solid background on the basic skills, they won't be able to absorb written information that's fundamental to later schooling. At best, they'll be forced to catch up all the way through school. At worst, they won't learn. That's bad for the children and bad for the profession.

An Elementary Teacher's Day

We ran through a typical day of an elementary school teacher back in Chapter 3 with Walter, the fourth-grade teacher. Here we will look at the day for a slightly more unusual class—Steve A.'s South Bronx third-graders.

Steve starts his day by driving down to the school from his home in Westchester County, a suburb of New York City. It's a half-hour commute under the best of circumstances, so Steve's on the road early. He tries to get to school while there is still a parking space available on the street near the school. Parking is difficult on these city streets, because there are far more cars than spaces. Late-arriving teachers end up double-parking or worse.

Steve walks directly into the school. He doesn't have much to fear from the neighborhood—he's nearly six feet tall and built like a dump truck—but the streets are not as pleasant or safe as in wealthier neighborhoods. His school is located about five blocks uptown from Yankee Stadium, in a medium-to-bad area. The school draws its students from two different neighborhoods—the highrise projects, where many of the families are on welfare, and some lower-middle-class highrise buildings. The school is about two-thirds black and one-third Hispanic.

Steve has learned over the past few years that it's necessary to keep an eye on what goes on around the school, so the children and the teachers remain safe and healthy. He doesn't like to have to call the police if someone who is not a student is hanging around the halls or grounds. He prefers to handle it "unofficially," and he usually convinces most trespassers that the halls of an elementary school are not the best place to hang out. But he has developed a sense of the danger level of every situation— a sort of "street sense"—and it's served him well up to now.

Today is just a normal day, with no undesirables lurking about in the halls or stairwells, and only one or two minor altercations to break up. Since the kids are still quite young—the oldest is 10 or 11—the fights are more adolescent "I'm badder than you are" jostling matches than real fights, like in the junior high and high schools.

Steve makes his way to his classroom and settles down on the edge of his desk to await his students. He maintains a very informal atmosphere in his classroom, because, he says, it fits in with the life-styles of most of his students.

This class was formed last year to group together all the children of the same age who had demonstrated behavior problems. Steve had volunteered to take that class of seven-year-olds, and he felt that it was such a success that he had volunteered for it again. But last year's class had been a special program, and the funds dried up, so the experimental class of seven-year-olds was canceled. Instead, the administration kept him with the same group of kids, plus a few extras, for third grade. It was the first time Steve had ever graduated along with his children.

The kids file in and take their seats. There's a definite routine by now, because Steve has made sure there would be. "I always put up a tough front at first, to establish some kind of order—which is pretty difficult in city schools. After a few weeks, I relax a little and let them relax, too." Especially with last year's class, he had had to establish order very quickly and firmly. He's found it helpful to establish definite rules for the class's behavior. He makes only a couple of rules, but he adheres to them strictly. The most important and useful of these is his "work now, play later" rule. It states very simply that when it's time to work, we work, and we'll be able to play later.

The children are surprisingly calm and relaxed, considering that some of them have been tagged with a "behavior problem" label. The strict but secure atmosphere seems to have done them good. There is, of course, a certain amount of laughing and talking, but this seldom gets out of hand or disruptive.

Steve walks around the classroom almost constantly as he teaches, and he's very tactile with his class—an arm around small shoulders here, a hand on the head there. It seems to physically calm these kinetic youngsters, and they pay more attention.

"Most of the kids in this school are slightly behind their grade level. In the past three years, it's gotten a bit worse, especially with reading. Some of my kids just can't read yet, and I have to spend a lot of time on it with them. It's something they must be able to do before they can do anything else."

The children work in very short lesson spurts, and Steve livens things up with conversation and jokes. The fact that he is serious about taking very little real disruption from them helps them understand exactly what is expected of them, when, and for how long. His teaching training did not prepare him for this type of teaching, so he had to figure it out as he went along. He has the advantage of being able to look very objectively at what he's attempting, and to make honest appraisals of his success. This way, he can throw out ways of teaching that don't work as well, and keep what seems to help.

He admits that his approach is not scientifically designed or carried out. "It's a custom approach to teaching, like how the auto-body shop builds a customized car. You start with something basic and add things or take things away until you have just what you need—for that particular car." His teaching approach is "customized" for this particular class of children. He has no guarantee that it will work for his next class, or for any other.

His class goes along very much like a conventional third-grade class, except for the shorter segments into which the day is broken up, and the slightly noisier atmosphere. Steve goes through reading, arithmetic, and health before the morning break. After recess, he does some more reading work with those who are having trouble, while keeping an eye on the rest of the class. He uses a variety of approaches to get his most intransigent nonreaders to learn to read. One little boy, Anthony, tells

Steve a story, which Steve writes down for him. Then it's Anthony's turn to read back his own story, with Steve's assistance. Juan is building sentences with word cards. Juan's special problem is that he doesn't hear much English spoken around his house, so he's not that familiar with how the words should sound. He speaks English well, but his foundation for relating spoken words to strings of letters is shaky.

Lunchtime for Steve is a free period. At one time, teachers were required to spend lunch, as well as the rest of the day, with their students. This was changed a couple of years ago through a contract-negotiating session between the board of education and the teachers' union.

After lunch, Steve separates the children into two groups. They're going to play a game that he's devised (to get them to write and work together). There are two teams competing to see which can devise the best "map" of the area, their neighborhood. He tells the groups to describe the streets, the stores, even the people, to show what's in the neighborhood. He gives them 20 minutes, because he figures that will be about as long as an organization structure will last. He shuttles between the two competing groups, watching to see how each works together, who makes the decisions, who does the writing, and what the students consider important about the neighborhood. There's a lot of raucous arguing and baiting between the two teams before they settle down to write their maps. Marinda immediately takes charge of one group and directs Anthony to write down the map. He complains that he can't spell, but they all shout him down, saying they'll tell him what to write. Steve smiles, thinking that this is just what he had hoped would happen. Alex, the oldest, and in some ways the meanest, child in the class, dominates the second group. He's a year-and-a-half older than most of his classmates, and he's used to getting his way. But he keeps making mistakes in the map which must be corrected by other members of the group. Soon, the members of his team stop deferring to him as much as usual, and the group is leaderless.

Steve calls time, and the two groups present their maps. Both have left out landmarks Steve would have considered important, but both groups have included many of the same things. Both maps say that Yankee Stadium is a few blocks away, and they both mention the recreation center in one of the nearby projects. These are obviously two important landmarks to these eight-year-olds.

After the map exercise, Steve picks a subject to calm the kids down, so they have music. Steve was not trained to teach singing—in fact, he was not even trained to sing—but he does a creditable job, and the children seem to enjoy his very involved singing style. By the time they finish music, they are getting restless, so it is good that the afternoon play period follows.

When they return to class, they practice more reading and spelling. As the end of this day nears, Steve's creative and physical energies are pretty much used up. The last bell rings and he says good-bye to his students, sending them home. Then he remembers he has a parent-principal meeting. He is not looking forward to this—that may be why he almost forgot it. But the principal insists that teachers and parents have frequent contact, and he is a very tough principal. His name is Mr. Swan, and all the teachers, as well as the students, call him that (no first names here). Steve goes to Mr. Swan's office to wait for Arturo's parents to arrive. Arturo's father works nights, and his mother works afternoons, so they are both making a special effort to meet and talk with Steve.

The meeting is very quiet, as these meetings go. Feelings sometimes run so high that Steve has heard of teachers being attacked by parents. "The major problem, especially in these community school board schools, is parents," Steve says. "They play power games like you wouldn't believe."

Arturo's mother wants to know how he's doing in arithmetic, because he had had some trouble with it in second grade. This year, Arturo's best friend, also in his class, is a good arithmetic student. They work together on their homework—something very rare in the third grade of this school. So Arturo's doing fine in arithmetic. And since he is doing well in his other subjects, there are no worries about his school work.

Arturo's parents and Steve part cordially, and Steve sighs his relief. If he could only stay with the kids and not have to meet their parents, he would be happy. Steve heads for his car to try to get on the road before the real rush hour begins. That's one thing he can do without, after a full day with 28 third graders.

Requirements for Elementary Teachers

The basic requirement for an elementary school teacher is a bachelor's degree in teaching, plus your state's teaching certificate. In a number of states, this is enough to get you a starting job.

Several states require that you complete a certain amount of graduate study in a specified period of time in order to keep your certification. In some areas, this may culminate in a requirement for a master's degree within a specified number of years.

Many people who want to teach elementary school continue straight through to their master's degrees. This approach has a lot to recommend it. Several states already require a master's, and more states will in the near future. And, of course, a master's degree gives you a competitive advantage over other candidates when you're applying for a job.

Some states phrase their requirements ambiguously. For example, one state requires "the equivalent of a bachelor's degree in elementary education," apparently to give the board of education some leeway to grant certification in special cases. But in reading the requirements that you obtain from the state board, interpret them strictly. In most cases, this will be the rule that's applied.

Requirements are growing stricter because there are more and more out-of-work teachers with advanced degrees. School boards have the luxury of choosing from among several well-qualified candidates.

Elementary teaching requires flexibility—sometimes a teacher must work with one or two children and keep an eye on the rest of the class at the same time.

Personal Characteristics

Every person who has anything to do with either teacher training or with schools has his/her very own list of necessary personality traits for an elementary school teacher. But the following is fairly representative.

We have mentioned the first characteristic before: patience. Frustrations abound in elementary school, with students, administrators, school boards, budgets, other teachers, even buses. It's difficult to get through a single day as a teacher without having your patience tried by at least one of these. You are allowed to lose patience with all but two—the children and the administration. Taking out your frustrations on a group of little children who can't fight back effectively is very destructive to them and to you. And venting your frustrations about the administration can get you into a lot of trouble.

A second characteristic is a love of learning. Children learn by example, and if you provide them with the example of a person who loves to find things out and to grow and expand his/her mind, they possibly may learn to become the same sort of people. This is the great goal of education. If you teach them nothing but this, you have taught them the most important lesson in education.

You must be able to work well with other professionals. Teaching is a cooperative effort. You must be able to work with the administration—the principal, assistant principal, the superintendent of schools, and others—and with your fellow teachers in order to coordinate your efforts to give the students the best and broadest educational experience possible. This may involve working through the administration office to schedule special activities for your students, working with counselors or a school psychologist to detect potential or actual problems in your students, and working with your fellow teachers to understand each child's special needs and to decide how best to serve them.

Your love of learning must include a good grasp of the subject matter you cover in class. Some people believe that you don't have to know very much about a subject to teach it to someone else. But in elementary school, you have to answer innumerable questions on what you are teaching at the moment. A teacher shouldn't have to say "I don't know" very often—it's bad for the image.

Job Opportunities

Currently, there are many more elementary school teachers than available jobs. Schools are encouraging teachers to retire early, and they're tightening their requirements for new teachers, either officially, by setting new certification requirements, or unofficially, by choosing only candidates who are slightly overqualified. In short, job opportunities are slim at the moment. The best chance of getting a job is in the "least desirable" school systems in ghetto or rural poor areas. Although many teachers are aware of the opportunities in these areas and there's no lack of applicants for open jobs, teachers stay in these jobs for shorter periods of time, so more vacancies come up per year.

It also helps to maximize your qualifications by getting one or more advanced degrees in either early childhood education, education, or psychology. These degrees, especially the doctorate, are looked on with favor by those who hire teachers.

7 HIGH SCHOOL TEACHER

High school teachers differ from the two types of teachers we have discussed so far because they usually teach a specific subject to changing groups of students, instead of a variety of subjects to the same group. These teachers cover grades seven through twelve or nine through twelve, depending on the school system. Their students range from the ages of 12 to 18. Because the teaching style is different than elementary school, the requirements for the job also differ slightly.

The Duties of a High School Teacher

A high school teacher's duties vary according to his/her special area of expertise. An English teacher covers writing and the understanding and appreciation of English literature. A math teacher is expert on the intricacies of algebra, geometry, trigonometry, calculus, and the like. Other high school study specialties include languages (French, Spanish, Latin, etc.), science (earth science, biology, etc.), history and social studies (ancient and modern history, sociology, civics), and various vocational and technical specialties.

High school teachers must cover the material specified by the school board in the required time, assign and grade homework, administer tests, and prepare various administrative reports. The duties may also include overseeing certain extracurricular activities, such as plays and clubs, the school yearbook and newspaper, various sports teams, and the school band. They also may chaperon at school-sponsored dances and the like. Extracurricular activities are among the most rewarding and yet the most time-consuming of a teacher's responsibilities. As a teacher, you'll have the opportunity to watch your students grow in ways other than academically. This is the time when most children are trying to become adults. You'll be placed in a position to help them make the transition. This responsibility is not contract-defined, but it is a duty, nevertheless.

A Day in the Life

Cal T. is a chemistry teacher in a small, private, boys' prep school in the South. He is much loved by his students and respected by his fellow teachers. He has worked as a teacher almost as long as he can remember, he claims.

His day starts shortly after the opening ceremonies that start each day at this school. His chemistry class is required of every student who graduates, so at some point he gets to teach each and every one of the 180 or so students who are in the school at any one time.

He goes to his office and dumps his rumpled jacket over his desk chair. He works in shirtsleeves because a jacket cramps his style. He enters the small lecture hall, which is adorned with a periodic table of the elements and a blackboard. For his three classes a day, he entertains, diagrams, demonstrates, drills, cajoles, and shouts knowledge of his first love—chemistry—into students' heads.

Today he is demonstrating the "clock reaction"—so called because it demonstrates that a mixture of chemicals in a certain balance can be "set" to change color after a specified period of time. This is a classic among high school science class demonstrations, because it is such a profound and startling illustration of the point the teacher is trying to make.

Three beakers of a clear liquid sit on the lab table in front of him. He takes a flask of another clear liquid and carefully pours a measured amount into each beaker. He then starts into his lecture about chemical equilibrium. He keeps an eye on his watch, noting that the first beaker is set to change color in three minutes. Almost to the second, the first beaker's liquid changes from clear to a deep purple. The students notice immediately and exchange appreciative glances. Cal pretends to be engrossed in his diagram at the blackboard. In another three minutes, the second beaker changes color. The change is sudden and startling. He continues talking, seemingly oblivious. Finally, he makes a grand flourish and points his chalk to the third beaker, which, right on cue, changes from clear to purple. He gets a round of applause.

When the applause dies down (nine people don't applaud very long—they get self-conscious), he goes on to show that the clock experiment is a good example of the principle of chemical equilibrium.

Cal likes to use demonstrations like these because they illustrate in very graphic form what he's trying to say in words and diagrams. High school students are notoriously flighty, and you have to keep them surprised and involved if you want to teach them anything.

Between classes, Cal spends time with students in his office. Some come in for extra help, which he's happy to give. He hates to see students having a hard time grasping the chemical principles he is trying to communicate. At times, he finds it necessary to ask one of his less-motivated students when his free periods are, so he can make an appointment with the student to put in some individual work.

Some students come in just to talk, because Cal is easy and fun to talk to and has a quick sense of humor. And three seniors are taking a special course with him in advanced biochemistry. They are now designing an experiment, which they'll later carry out under his supervision and write up, thesis-style, as their final project. They seem to be in his office almost constantly.

At lunchtime, he walks over to his house in the faculty housing on the edge of the campus. He lunches with his four-year-old and his wife before returning for afternoon classes. He repeats the same class, with some variations, for each of his three groups of chemistry students.

At 3:10, when all the other teachers have finished classes for the day, Cal supervises the chemistry labs. His students are in the lab till well after 4:30, working on their qualitative analysis projects. One minor emergency occurs when a student jabs his hand with a broken piece of glass tubing. Cal sends him to the infirmary, and uses the occurrence to demonstrate again the proper way to push glass tubing through a rubber stopper. This is one technique the students consistently seem incapable of learning.

Later in the afternoon, he holds a special makeup session in balancing chemical equations for a group of boys who just can't seem to grasp the principle. This goes on till almost dinnertime.

Cal goes home with a load of papers and project reports under his arm. He sits at the kitchen table after dinner, going over papers and planning the next week's classes. Around 7:00, he gets a semi-hysterical telephone call from a student begging help on the second homework problem. Cal answers by asking a series of leading questions until the student understands the underlying principle behind the problem. This is a small but significant victory; this student has had great difficulty realizing chemistry's importance to the world and, worse still, he didn't see that it had an internal order and sense to it—before tonight.

Cal goes back to grading papers. All in a day's work.

Not every high school teacher has a day as idyllic and simple as this, but many of the teaching characteristics are the same. In virtually every high school, the day is broken up into periods, and most teachers teach the same class several times a day to different groups of students. Some teachers teach several different but related classes, like first- and second-year French, or medieval and American history. Most of the rest of the teacher's day is taken up with individual student consultations or with special activities with various student groups—the French club, sports teams, debating team, and the like. Many of these activities take place during after-school hours.

Some schools reimburse teachers for extracurricular assistance to students. The pay is highest for coaching the football and basketball teams, and it ranges on down the list through various other sports, the band, music instruction, dramatics and debating, the yearbook and newspaper, and sponsoring the cheerleaders. This pay does not represent a lot of money, by any means. According to Educational Research Service, Inc.,

In high school, teachers often specialize in one or two particular subjects, like math or science.

the highest pay ($1,396 in 1975–76) for extracurricular activity sponsors went to football coaches.

Job Requirements

As in other areas of teaching, the basic requirement is the bachelor's degree. In every case, the bachelor's degree is in education, with a certifiable emphasis in the subject area being taught (science, math, a foreign language). But many school districts now require a master's degree of their high school teachers. The same forces work upon high school teaching jobs as upon other jobs; there are now fewer students, so fewer teachers are needed. Thus educational requirements are upped, either formally or informally.

Every school district, whatever the variations among them, requires that their teachers have an "education in education" before they can be certified to teach.

One important requirement that you must not overlook is the continuing education requirement. You must remain current in your field by taking refresher courses in your specific subject area. Some school districts require this refresher course every few years, and more will follow the practice as it becomes more popular.

Personal Characteristics

You guessed it: patience. But by the high school years the need for a teacher's patience might be more appropriately termed "tolerance." High-school-age youngsters are in the midst of powerful changes, physically, psychologically, and socially. They start the ninth grade as children, and they graduate twelfth grade as adults.

This great change brings with it all sorts of strange behaviors. Kids you loved last year will become monsters, hating you, hating your class, hating school, and hating themselves. This is usually temporary, but that's cold comfort for a teacher who goes through someone else's adolescence over and over again.

At first, your students appear to be children, trapped in adult bodies. Later, they become adults, trapped in children's bodies. This split personality is the source of all the problems. But whatever the source, the students need understanding and tolerance so they can get through this phase with a minimum of stress.

Another important quality for a teacher of this age group is maturity or self-respect. Young people are closely attuned to the vibrations of a shaky self-concept, because they are going through their own examination of the self. They will home in on a teacher who lacks self-respect, and that will be the end of any order or discipline, much less learning, in his/her class.

One last quality is difficult to describe by any name other than wisdom. A high school teacher needs the perspective and experience to help students go through their changes without putting his/her own problems and unresolved conflicts into their lives. You have to be able to say to a student who's come to you with a problem, "This is a real problem you're facing, but it will pass, and you will grow up to be a whole adult." And when students have problems that *won't* go away with age—problems like drug abuse or unwanted pregnancies—teachers should also be equipped to help them. It's a narrow path to tread. Teachers are in a position to know a lot about their students, because of the time they spend with them. They may even know more about their students than the students' parents do. And teachers must exercise judgment and caution, so that whatever they do, their students will be better for it.

Opportunities for High School Teaching Jobs

The effects of the student population decline are already being felt at high school level. The slight increases forecast for the mid to late 1980's will hit the high schools closer to the late '80's than to the middle. Any expansion of job opportunities will have to wait till then.

Even so, there are some areas of high school teaching which have greater opportunities than others. The sciences and math are examples. A recent school board publication illustrates the current situation for teachers. It tells of a young woman with a master's degree in early childhood education who has been named to fill the vacant post of teacher's aide, and a young man with a bachelor's degree in chemistry who has been named to replace a retiring chemistry teacher. The difference is clear: It's easier to get a job in the sciences than in elementary education. It's a shame that this very qualified young woman is forced to take a job whose only requirement is a high school education. But the young chemistry teacher, with two years' less education, currently has greater opportunities for employment than she does.

Other opportunities exist in the more specialized areas of high school teaching, such as resource-room teacher and vocational and technical teacher. These specialties have educational and experiential requirements that set them apart from other high school specialties.

8 SPECIAL EDUCATION TEACHER

Although every child has special educational needs, some children's needs are greater than others. Children with learning disabilities, physical handicaps, mental retardation, all need the assistance of a teacher specially trained to help them learn in the best possible way. And children who are emotionally disturbed require carefully trained professionals to ease their way into a normal and healthy life. Some children are more intellectually gifted than their classmates. These children, too, need a specialist trained to assist them to reach their potential.

These teachers are trained in what is known as special education. Recently, the definition of special education has been expanded to include services such as speech pathology and correction and special reading instruction.

Another specialist, whose job has been developed within the past decade, is the resource-room teacher. S/he is in charge of providing special learning resources, especially in high school, for students with unusual educational needs.

Learning Disabilities Specialist

This professional is involved with testing, identifying, and providing a special educational environment for learning-disabled children. S/he may have contact with a great number of children in carrying out the first two responsibilities, even though only a small percentage of these children will require continuing services—those who are identified as having a learning disability. A "learning disability" is a physical, perceptual, intellectual, or emotional handicap that keeps a child from understanding information or concepts. This may take the form of such exotic disorders as dyslexia, in which the child scrambles the order of letters on a page so the words make no sense ("saw" may look like "was" or "swa"). Other disabilities are less easily diagnosed.

A teacher trained to recognize learning disabilities is in a discipline of teaching that is relatively new. Until perhaps 15 years

Teachers of learning-disabled children must have special training to understand and help these children with their special learning needs.

ago, children with learning disabilities were classified as "slow learners," instead of as perfectly intellectually capable children who nevertheless couldn't understand information presented to them. Various other disabilities are still being "discovered" with the aid of new testing methods and experiments — all in the hope of helping a greater percentage of our nation's children profit from their school experience.

Physical Handicaps Specialist

These teachers may or may not have physical handicaps themselves, but they must be able to understand the nature and limiting forces of a child's handicap. Even more important, they must avoid overestimating the limitations posed by a child's handicap. People can overcome tremendous odds, but if those who are trained to help them assume that they are unable to help themselves, their task is much more difficult.

The range of handicaps includes blindness (either partial or total), hearing loss, loss of muscular coordination, mobility problems (such as being confined to a wheelchair or requiring crutches to get around), and a great number of other disabilities. Teachers must be able to assist these children in coping with, and sometimes overcoming, their handicaps. They also must be trained to use the proper emotional attitude to be the most help to their young charges.

Mental Retardation Specialist

Mentally retarded children are unable to understand their world at a level close to what is appropriate to their age group. Mildly retarded children are often placed in a regular classroom because they develop best with children their own age who are not disabled.

But children whose intellectual capacities are far below their age level usually do better with a specially trained teacher in a special classroom. This teacher must be carefully trained to provide the best possible learning and social environment for the children.

A mental retardation professional cannot relate completely to the experiences and feelings of a retarded child, because someone who can attain that degree of training is not retarded. But it's necessary that a person who teaches retarded children be able to understand their charges' emotions. Some retarded children exhibit behavior problems, which must be dealt with compassionately and with the interests of the child in mind.

Teachers of mentally retarded children may work in public schools, in special publicly supported schools, in private schools, or in public or private live-in facilities. Their students range in age from birth on up to young adulthood.

Teacher of Emotionally Disturbed Children

The professional who teaches emotionally disturbed children is part of a team. S/he is in partnership with doctors, social workers, psychologists, physical therapists, and sometimes even the police and the courts. This type of teaching by and large takes place in special schools, either public or private.

There is a wide variety of emotional disturbances, with a bafflingly broad range of symptoms, causes, and treatment. A specialist in emotional disturbances must have an extensive background in psychology especially geared to the age of the children being taught, and in some cases geared to the special type of disturbance.

This is a particulary difficult yet rewarding branch of special education. Here the opportunity to change someone's life for the better is a daily fact. And the possibility of failure is another fact. There are many failures for each success, but teachers who stay in this area believe the value of the successes offsets the failures. It isn't a job for the weakhearted, who must be rewarded at every turn. For them, a regular classroom would prove more suitable. This job is for those who can appreciate small gains and minimize losses, build on strengths and cope with weaknesses.

Many emotionally disturbed children have a tremendous need to be nurtured and taken care of. Some may be extremely intelligent children who cannot cope with a regular classroom or traditional schooling. Others may have severe learning disabilities, or they may be mentally retarded. But what unifies these students into one group is their inability to deal with the world in a healthy and productive way.

They may or may not be a danger to others and to themselves. They may be extremely disruptive, demanding your attention every moment. They may be so withdrawn that they do not respond to your approaches, or they may live in a fantasy world of their own invention. Each child requires a different approach and offers different possibilities for success, however you define that word.

Judy has been a teacher of emotionally disturbed, learning-disabled children for the past eight years. She works in what is known as a "cottage school," where most of the children live and are supervised 24 hours a day.

"This year, I have a class of all boys who live at home. It's a big improvement over the live-in classes, because the kids are still in some kind of home environment, whatever its faults. I teach a group of six 11- and 12-year-olds. They're mostly referrals from the city schools, because their teachers couldn't cope with their disruptions.

"There have been some big changes lately because of different federal rules for the education of handicapped kids. Many of the boys who would have come to us under earlier guidelines are now being 'mainstreamed'—kept in the regular classroom. It's very tough for those schools.

"When I first came here, I was much more idealistic. But when you see the same type of child year after year—deprived, psychotic, guiltless, unable to respond on a human level—you realize that you're not about to 'save' those children. You become more realistic. You try to see what good you *can* do for these kids. If you lack nurturing in the first two years of life, you've got a very tough situation. And that's exactly what's happened with most of these boys. They've never learned to relate, and if you don't learn it during that crucial relationship-forming period, your chances of learning it at all aren't too good.

"I have a full-time aide to help me with these six kids, and they're still a handful. We have a regular schoolday—spelling, reading, art, music, lunch, gym, math. We have to maintain a very structured environment. The kids have no inner control, and so we have to be very aware of things constantly. You can't kid or tease with these kids—they can't deal with abstractions. They think very concretely. There was a good example of this yesterday. My aide had said something on Friday about how he was going away to Death Valley—jokingly. When he walked in on Monday, one of the kids asked him, "What are you doing here? You said you were going away." You can't ever make threats that most kids wouldn't take seriously. You can't say, "I'll cut your finger off if you steal Joey's pencil again." The kid might be very frightened, and it could damage whatever relationship you might have with him.

"The thing that divides us from regular teachers is that we get no feedback from the kids. There's no ability in them to respond. They're so needful—there's a personal vacuum inside them. When you write a math problem on the board for them to work, suddenly six hands are up in the air, begging you to come sit beside them and help with the problem. They demand so much personal attention.

"And academic accomplishment to them means nothing. But some of the kids who can read like it. One of our most important tasks is to teach them to read. All the reading machines and fancy texts in the world won't get them to learn. It takes sitting down with them and *teaching* them. I do get a kick out of it when a kid learns to read, even a little.

"It is a much easier job in terms of preparation level. A regular fourth-grade teacher has to do a lot more before-class preparation. My school runs from nine to three, and that's about all the time I have to put into it, besides paperwork.

"The paperwork is extensive, but I don't really mind it. We have to fill out what's called an Individual Education Prescription for each child—it runs to about fourteen pages. But a lot of the preparation involved is notes I would be taking anyway, just to be at my best in the classroom.

"The one really negative part of the whole job is meeting with the parents. We're required by law to do this at specified intervals to talk over the child's progress and special problems. But quite a few—I'd say most—of these parents are as emotionally disturbed as their kids. That's why the kids are here in the first place. It's okay if they're relatively quiet, but some of them are really paranoid, and they start yelling about how their child's been taken from them, that it's a conspiracy to hurt them, that they're going to come and kill you. I could do without that.

"I want to stay with this job. The atmosphere is looser than in most schools, and I like my colleagues. You have to approach the classroom almost clinically—you can't expect to work miracles, just do what you can."

Specialist for Gifted Children

This is a comparatively recent specialty. Formerly, especially intelligent children were thought to do well in school, period. Nobody really imagined that there might be a better way of educating them to develop their special gifts. This attitude is slowly changing. Teachers of gifted children are working in another vanguard area, doing research as they teach. They are developing and testing new teaching methods to see exactly what works and why it works to give these children the best possible learning environment.

Often, exceptional children have a particular gift or talent in one area. They may be brilliant in math or science or they may compose music like Mozart did at the age of three. The task of their teachers is to make sure this gift is not developed at the expense of the rest of the child's personality and abilities. It's an interesting and challenging area of work.

Reading Specialist

Reading specialists help children who are having trouble learning to read and are falling behind their grade level in these skills. This may be due to a whole range of causes, physical, such as visual impairment, or psychological, and the reading teacher must be trained to detect the specific reason for the child's inability to learn to read. Once the cause is determined, the reading teacher provides special treatment. S/he often works with the child's regular classroom teacher in planning out the best approach. And s/he may work with other professionals, like doctors or social workers, to provide more comprehensive services to the child.

Resource-Room Teacher

Resource-room teachers are specialists in learning disabilities as well. They work in the regular public schools, providing services to those students who need special help.

Susan was a resource-room teacher until very recently. She recalls her main responsibilities to her students.

"My job was to make sure they succeeded. They were so used to failing by the time they got to high school—even a small success was important. I had high school kids who couldn't read, couldn't carry on conversations with other students, couldn't remember their assignments. One major battle I had was to get the regular teachers to write the next day's assignment on the board. Kids with learning disabilities don't learn or remember the first time you say something. So the kids would be leaving the room, and the teacher would yell out something like, 'Do the last three problems on page 76.' Well, my kids can't get that to stay in their heads. They'll get the wrong assignment, or forget there even was an assignment.

"As a special teacher, you can't go to the other teachers and tell them they have to change how they're teaching because your kid can't keep up. You say, 'What can I do to help you? I want to make your job as easy as possible, so tell me what Frank needs to know for each day's assignment.' That's a non-threatening approach. The other way is a threatening approach, and you won't do anything but antagonize the other teacher.

"I quit for two reasons. First, I'm going to architecture school, which is something I've wanted to do for several years. Second, I was getting overloaded. I had too many kids assigned to me, and way too much paperwork. It became a 24-hour-a-day job. I'd sit awake at night and try to figure out how to solve Brian's or Beth's problem. I was compulsive about it."

Job Requirements

Requirements for a special education certificate are almost universally the master's degree, although some states will give certification to applicants with a B.A. in special education. The requirements grow stricter as the field becomes more common to public school and as the duties become more appreciated for the background they require.

Different colleges offer different specializations, and you should look into a school's programs carefully to make sure you can get the specific training you want.

Some states also require that you have some experience on a special certification before you are granted a permanent (or renewable) certification. Contact the state board of education where you plan to teach to get the most current information.

Personal Characteristics

In this branch of teaching especially, an acceptance of personal differences among people is necessary. Most special education teachers teach children who are different from the run-of-the-mill public school student. The students' abilities or behavior will be significantly different from the norm, and you must be able to accept, even welcome this.

You need the ability to work easily with other people. Children with special needs are often involved with the various social service branches of local government, either because of their behavior problems, family or economic problems, or their requirements for special services. You as a teacher will work together for the children with representatives of these social service organizations, and with physical therapists, rehabilitation counselors, psychologists, psychiatrists, and other medical personnel.

Finally, you must have a willingness to learn, to expand your knowledge of your field, your world, and yourself. This ability will enable you to provide the very best teaching for those children who need it most.

Employment Opportunities

Employment opportunities in special education are closely linked to federal laws, rules, court decisions, and grant money. For example, when the Federal Office of Education ruled that local school districts had a responsibility to provide for children with learning disabilities, suddenly a whole range of jobs opened up for people with this training. If you are interested in special education, you can enter a master's program in the general area and pick a specialty as job opportunities demand. You need not make your final decision at the moment you enter graduate school.

In general, opportunities in this area are highly variable. There are good years and bad years—sometimes many graduates take jobs they are overqualified for, and sometimes most of them manage to get just the job they have been trained for and desire.

It is most important to get into a college that has an active network of contacts among those who do the hiring. Often, a superintendent or department head will call his old school to find out if the placement office has anyone to fill a certain job. Many teaching jobs are filled this way—nobody even hears about the job until after it is filled.

A good gauge of a college's network of contacts is its age and size. The older the college, the more graduates it is likely to have "in the field" and the more chances you will have of hearing of a job. Graduates of a particular school represent the college in two ways: (1) They move into positions of responsibility where they are able to make decisions about who gets hired, and (2) they act as representatives of the style of teaching taught at the particular college, so administrators know what they are getting when they hire another graduate.

A last gauge of a college's effectiveness in placing you when you graduate is its name and fame. As you talk to people about teaching and colleges, a few names will come up often enough to give you an idea of which schools are best known. Graduating from a "name" college is a psychological foot in the door. You can't measure the effect, but it's there. Of course, that's not a reason to make a final choice on a college, but it is one thing you should consider.

If you are interested in going into the field of special education, it is a good idea to keep up with current legislation regarding education. Special education is one discipline that has profited through government actions, and many "special ed" positions today owe their existence to decisions of the courts, Congress, and the executive branch.

9 VOCATIONAL AND TECHNICAL TEACHERS

Vocational and technical teachers are those teachers who teach their students a trade so they can go directly from school to the workforce. This is one of the major factors that separates vocational teachers from academic-subject teachers. The other major factor is that, in most cases, trades teachers must have experience in actually *doing* what they teach. Thus, someone who teaches drafting must have worked as a draftsman or architect for a specified number of years.

Duties of a Vocational or "Tech" Teacher

Of course, the duties performed vary by the subject taught but, in most cases, the major duty is simple: give the students enough information and experience so they can do the job they are being trained to do. Other responsibilities are the same as those of other teachers. They assign homework, grade papers, give tests, direct student projects, and work with the administration.

Vocational teachers may have more contact with guidance counselors than most other teachers to keep them up to date on opportunities in their particular fields. Otherwise, they interact with their colleagues in normal "teacherly" ways.

One duty of all teachers which is especially necessary for a "tech" teacher is the requirement that s/he keep up with developments in his or her field. This may mean maintaining a business office while teaching in a school, or taking courses to advance knowledge of new methods or discoveries.

Types of Vocational Teachers

The general category of "vocational teacher" breaks down into several divisions. The following list is by no means exhaustive; every school district will have some types of teachers not on the list and will be missing others.

Tech teachers teach a wide range of technical subjects that go beyond the traditional trade school subjects of auto mechanics and metal shop work. They may teach anything from chemical engineering to computer science. And, of course, they must be experienced in whatever they are teaching.

Industrial arts teachers teach certain industrial skills, such as auto mechanics and body work, carpentry, metal shop work, and several other crafts and trades that have been taught almost as long as there have been unions and apprentice programs. Often, the high school industrial arts course prepares a student to enter an apprentice program immediately upon graduation, thus sometimes skipping one or more years of the prescribed apprentice program.

This particular educational program was designed well before the Second World War to provide boys (at that time) with jobs upon graduation and to provide industry with skilled labor. It can be considered the forerunner of most other tech and trade programs.

Home economics teachers teach students to run a home and, by extension, teach them skills that will get them jobs, if that is what they seek. Skills included are child care, sewing, food preparation, and health care. Other topics considered are social change, marital and family relations, and population growth.

Distribution and sales teachers teach students how to work in sales and purchasing for large or small merchandising firms. Students may become buyers for department stores, floor sales people, or commission sales people.

Nursing teachers prepare their students to enter a nursing school or other health service training program. Their graduates may eventually become registered nurses, licensed prac-

Vocational and technical teachers may teach anything from printing press operation to cooking.

tical nurses, physical therapists, and doctors of various specialties.

Business ed. teachers instruct their students in the proper ways to run a business, whatever its size. Junior Achievement businesses are often set up and run by the business education class, under the direction of the business ed. teacher. Graduates may become managers, business administrators, or entrepreneurs.

Agriculture teachers often are found in rural areas teaching their students animal husbandry, agriculture, large-scale farming methods, practical biology and chemistry, and a variety of other topics related to modern agriculture. Their students are destined to become farmers or farm managers, forest and parks service employees, and veterinarians.

An Architecture and Design Teacher's Day

Sal M. is a practicing architect with his own design and construction firm. He's also a full-time teacher. In Sal's case, it's hard to tell at which job he's moonlighting.

He teaches in a specialized technical and trade high school, which he graduated from about 15 years ago. The school is now a rather run-down old building located in a rather run-down neighborhood. Sal's students go without proper supplies because of a combination of rapidly rising paper costs and rapidly declining materials budgets. He says he's still operating on a 1973 budget, even though materials have increased in cost nearly 200 percent since then.

"The vocational and technical teaching area is very close-knit. There are about 35 or 40 tech teachers in my entire city, out of about 1,600 teachers. In this state, you have to have a good amount of experience before they'll let you teach technical subjects, and you can't get teaching certification permanently until you've taught at least two years. So they're pretty careful about whom they hire. Other states, I can't speak for.

"The pay is pretty good for a teacher, because a tech teacher gets four or five years' credit for his work experience, and that moves him up along the pay scale a few notches. Even so, most of the people who take these jobs have to take a cut in income, at least at first. A union carpenter might be getting eight or ten bucks an hour—that's a lot more than a teacher's going to make. But we do it because we profited from it ourselves when we were kids. I graduated from this very school. There's no way I'd be where I am now if I hadn't gotten the education I did here. I just want to pass it along to others."

Sal starts his day visiting a construction site that his company is working on. It is 6:30. The sun has not yet cut the ice in the air. He confers with his site manager, then gets into his car for the 50-minute drive into town to the school. He regrets that he can't spend more time on his business—it's only been in operation for two years now, since he got his architect's license.

His first class is period one, so he can't afford to be late. Students are already sitting at drawing tables working on their final projects when he walks in.

"May I have your attention, please! The teacher has entered! Repeat, the teacher has entered!" He walks to a locker along the wall and hangs up his coat and scarf. He teaches this class in two parts—one part theory (taught as a lecture) and one part practical experience (taught as a lab). The students roll up their drawings and take out notebooks. This is the first part of the class, and he expects them to pay attention to what he says. He lectures for most of a class period on how to read electrician's notes on a blueprint. It is crucial that designers know how to read and use this system common in the design and construction work world.

The bell rings, and Sal reminds the students that they have two more weeks to finish their projects. They file out, and another group comes in for their lab period. They go straight to work, and he goes from one table to another, quietly making comments, suggestions, and answering questions. These two scenes are repeated twice more during the course of the day.

At lunchtime, he calls his site foreman to see how the work is coming. He learns that a man has been taken to the hospital with a steel fragment imbedded in his cheek. He had been pounding on a carpenter's hammer with another hammer, trying to dig the claws into a piece of wood to pry out a stubborn nail. The hammer had shattered, shooting him with a piece of steel as though he'd been shot. Sal's only comment is, "He's lucky it wasn't an inch higher." But he is frustrated that he is unable to keep on top of things like he would if he ran his business full time. He finds that somehow he's able to juggle two very demanding jobs only with the help of a teaching assistant who takes over some lab periods and a business partner and employees he can trust.

After school, he coaches a basketball team, and his kids are having a game today. The gym is filled with screaming teenagers as his team goes down to defeat before a group of much larger and stronger boys. But the attitude among the spectators is supportive—this school is a close-knit group, too.

Sal is very happy with his teaching job, and he doesn't even think about quitting. "This job has a lot of rewards. You get a great rapport going with the kids—they know you're the man who *does it* and you're teaching it to them. They *know* that what you do is important—it could end up being their livelihood. It's tough to show why a kid should study music or literature during an economic crisis. But vocational training has automatic accountability—a kid graduates and he does or does not get a job. You know when you've done him some good."

Job Requirements

Vocational teachers must be able to show that they know how to do what it is they teach by documenting their experience in the field. Many states require a minimum number of years at work in a particular field before you can qualify to teach it. In some cases, this may be all you have to demonstrate, besides the ability to deal with administrative paperwork. Some states allow you to teach vocational courses with nothing more than a high school education.

Personal Characteristics

Since, as a trades teacher, you may not have been taught how to present yourself before a group of students, you should be able to comfortably talk to a group of people in an understandable and clear way. Although you may be experienced at what you are talking about, your students are not, and you must be able to see when they are not getting what you are saying.

You should also be willing and able to give special attention to students who need it. They may not even realize they need your help until it's almost too late, so you should be sensitive to the learning processes and diagnose their needs before they run into trouble.

Job Opportunities

Vocational education is a growing field. There are more job opportunities here than in many other areas of teaching, at least proportionately. The actual number of job openings is small, however, because trade and vocational teachers represent a small percentage of all teachers.

The field should continue to grow, and opportunities will exist for people from many different walks of life to come into teaching and to show students how to do what they themselves do for a living.

10 ADMINISTRATIVE JOBS

Nearly every state in the nation requires that school principals have actual teaching experience for at least a short period of time, usually about two years. This means that virtually every school principal, not to mention every superintendent of schools, was at one time a teacher.

Climbing the organizational ladder in a conventional office sense is one of the only ways a teacher can truly advance from one position to another. Administrative jobs, such as principal, appeal to the small group of teachers who want to set educational policy for an entire school rather than teach a group of children and carry out policies determined by someone else.

The principal is the chief administrator of a school (sometimes more than one school). Teachers answer to him/her for their job performance, and students come to the principal's office for disciplinary and other matters affecting the efficient running of the school. Some principals may also teach, especially in a small school.

Principals answer to the superintendent of schools, an administrator selected by the local board of education to oversee the entire district's schools.

Duties of a School Administrator

A closer look at the principal's job may shed more light on the responsibilities of a school administrator. The principal supervises the entire operation of a school and oversees the work of the building maintenance, office, and teaching staff. S/he may have various assistants or deans, depending on the complexity of the school's administration.

The principal's office handles all complaints lodged by student against student, student against teacher, teacher against student, and teacher against teacher. S/he also must deal with the outside community on behalf of the school, including parents of students and surrounding residents complaining,

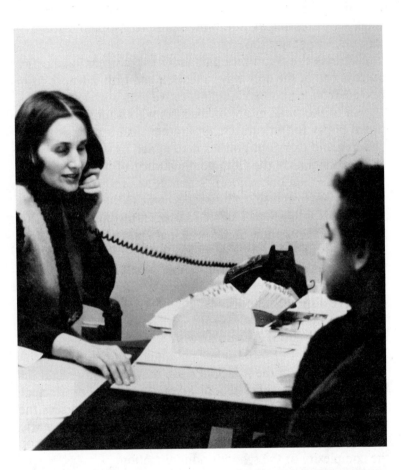

School principals spend a large part of their day dealing with the problems of individual students.

perhaps, about student behavior. It is also within the principal's duties to deal with more serious problems, such as student drug abuse. At times, these matters may involve the police or other outside agencies.

Job Requirements for Administrators

School administrators, from assistant principal up to school superintendent, are required in most cases to have at least a master's degree in education. Some states require the doctorate or its equivalent in course work. And as we mentioned, virtually all administrators must have a certain number of years of "successful" teaching at the grade level of the school they supervise. In addition, most states require that a certain portion of the graduate education be in school administration. Some graduate schools offer a master's degree in that area for those who want to become school administrators.

Personal Characteristics

A high regard for education must be the first characteristic of a successful school administrator. This philosophy should affect every decision s/he makes. In this way, the goal of public education can be realized: to have a well-informed and critical population able to decide intelligently on issues that affect our country.

A good school administrator should also have the characteristics of a successful administrator in business or government: the ability to take charge of a situation and make quick, accurate decisions; to keep open lines of communication to and from the various departments of the school; and to be flexible in and responsive to situations as they change from day to day. And a good school principal should have one more ability: to be compassionate and understanding toward students and staff.

Job Opportunities

Compared to the number of teachers, there are very few principals and other administrators. And the numbers of positions are decreasing, because schools are being closed or merged into one another.

The best administrative opportunities are in the same areas as the best teaching opportunities—in the "problem" schools in rural areas and inner-city ghettos. If you are "tough" enough and can affect these schools, your presence can be tremendously beneficial to the students, the faculty, and the school district.

11 TEACHER AIDE

One job in teaching requires no more than a high school education: a teacher aide. This nonprofessional education worker has a variety of duties, few of which usually require education courses. The position is relatively new in public education, and it is hard to say if the field will expand or to predict how many schools will employ aides.

A Teacher Aide's Duties

Aides take over routine noneducational and some educational duties so teachers have more time to concentrate on what they're trained to do—teach. Aides may handle simple paperwork, for example, such as take attendance or carry messages or forms to the office. They may work directly with children under the teacher's supervision, giving special attention to the reading needs of one child, helping another understand a math problem, look up research materials, or take charge of the repetitive drilling necessary for some children to master a necessity, such as the multiplication table. In addition s/he may handle much of a teacher's secretarial needs, such as running off tests on the duplicator, typing up reports, filing student records, grading test papers, and collecting homework.

In some specialized schools, the duties may be more involved. In a school for emotionally disturbed children, an aide may help the teacher keep order in the classroom, or work one-to-one with individuals who are having temporary difficulties. These aides may be required to have some educational training or experience with children.

Job Requirements

There is a wide variation in job requirements for teacher aide. Many schools require only a high school education. Personal qualities are often more important determining factors.

Teacher aides take over some of the duties of the classroom teacher to provide the teacher with some free time or with more productive teaching time.

You should be able to communicate well with the students and the teacher. You should be able to handle children and deal with difficult situations calmly. You must be able to follow directions and work closely with the teacher you're assigned to.

Some specific jobs require further education, depending on the duties. Some school districts also require some college experience, or an A.A. degree, or even a B.A.

Job Opportunities

Again, opportunities vary widely. Larger school districts and urban area schools are more likely to employ teacher aides. Some aides are funded through federal grants to school districts.

Although most teacher aide positions do not *require* higher education, the opportunities are greatest for those with the most education. The best way to find out if there are jobs in your area is to research locally. Contact the local board of education and ask if the schools are hiring teacher aides. Find out if there are any economic restrictions on who can become an aide (some grants limit employment to those under a certain economic level). Finally, ask what education level is required of applicants.

12 THE JOB HUNT

Let's look ahead a few years. You've finished college. You have a degree or two and a teaching certificate (if you're lucky). Now what? You can't sit in your room and wait for someone to discover you. You will have to help a little. Actually, you will have to help a lot, if you want to get discovered and hired.

The job-hunting approach outline below reflects the philosophy outlined in a wonderful book, *What Color Is Your Parachute?*

First Things First

Many teacher hopefuls closet themselves in a room during the last semester of college and fire off hundreds of resumes to school districts all over the country. This is wasteful and inefficient. Considering postal costs, it's also expensive. You have to do your homework first if you want to make a productive and efficient search for job possibilities. And the first thing you must answer is, "Where do I want to teach?" You may think it's chancy to limit your choices like that at the beginning. Why restrict yourself?

Well, what you are looking for here is more than a job. You are looking for a job that will make you happy and that will keep you satisfied, not to mention fed and clothed, for at least several years. If your job is going to do that, you are going to have to control as many aspects of the choice as you can.

This is the point when you must really level with yourself. If you have lived in Cedar Rapids all your life and want to stay there, it's silly to start by applying to schools in Trenton, New Jersey. On the other hand, Cedar Rapids may be the last place on earth you want to spend your life. Then don't apply for a job there.

You may want to spend your vacations skiing. Then seriously consider applying for a job in the Rockies. Don't ignore leisure-time activities that are important to you. One young teacher

It's a good idea to talk to teachers who already work in a school where you'd like to be hired.

loved the New York theater. She took a teaching job in a suburb in Southern California. The weather was beautiful, the money was good, she made friends. But she missed the Broadway shows. She finally moved back East, for less money and a less pleasant work environment. But she was happy in a way she couldn't be when she was away from what she loved.

Second question: What kind of school do you want to work in? Urban? Suburban? Rural? Large, or small? Ungraded or traditional? Public school or private school? A "challenging" school? What kind of challenges do you want to deal with in your job? Do you want sweet kids who will achieve for you, or tough kids who need a firm hand to guide them?

If you can answer these questions with some firmness, you'll be much farther along the road to finding the job you want than you may realize. What you are doing is fitting the school to your qualifications, instead of trying to fit your qualifications to a particular school. The result is, in some ways, the same—a job whose requirements you fill—but you haven't bent your personality out of shape to fit it.

By now, you have narrowed down your list of target schools to a few dozen. Your next assignment is crucial—you have to research the schools as thoroughly as you can. Learn who the students are and what kinds of neighborhoods they come from. Find out what problems the district has been having. Every school district has problems, and these problems almost always are reported in the local papers.

If possible, talk to teachers who work in the schools. Tell them you are looking for a teaching job. Tell them what kinds of challenges you're prepared to handle. Ask probing questions. Do you have to play politics with the department chairman? How is morale among the teachers? Who's retiring? Who has clout in determining who gets hired? Is there a strong administration to count on, or are teachers on their own? Are there student disciplinary problems? Is it a safe school? Is there a lot of red tape? How long does it take to get a light bulb replaced in a classroom fixture?

You have *not* sent in a resume yet; you're collecting the *school's* resume. By this time, you've trimmed your list of target schools significantly. Some are too dangerous or too old and depressing. Some are being phased out and merged with other schools. For whatever reasons, you've centered on a few schools which suit your interests, preferences, and desires.

Try to find out the name of the person who has the authority to hire you. This may be the principal, the superintendent of schools, or some other individual. This is the person you have to talk to now. Make a phone call. You're not going to ask him/her for a job. You're just going to talk. You're a student who's graduating soon, or you're an ex-teacher who's thinking of returning to the profession. You would like to come by for some advice. The school has a good reputation, and you want to see how things are run in the "real world." This should be very flattering to the person you're calling, not to mention a welcome break from the day's hectic routine. Make an appointment to come in and talk.

By now, you should be able to talk about the school as well as if you had worked there for a few years. You know the budgetary woes, the teachers' concerns, the false fire alarms and vandalism. These are the things on the principal's mind. And these are the things you're going to talk about, very seriously. This is going to be a cordial talk between two professionals about common interests. Of course, one of the two of you has more experience, and you have come to learn.

Since this school reflects your main interests—you've chosen it for just that reason—you shouldn't have any trouble holding up your end of the conversation.

After you've talked to the person in charge at each of your target schools, you should have enough information to decide which one seems best for you. Now is the time to begin overtures for a job. Choose the one or two schools you would really like to work in, and send a letter to the person in charge. Remind him/her of your conversation, say you were very impressed with the school and that you would like to be considered for a staff position, and ask if s/he would like to see your resume. Indicate that you think you could contribute to the school and to the students it serves. Follow up a couple of weeks later with a phone call, asking if the letter has been received and if you can answer any questions.

If all has gone well, and there is an opening, you should get a job. You've certainly done everything in your power to ensure it.

The Response

You may get a number of different responses from the schools you approach. The most disappointing is probably no answer at all. This kind of rudeness is not common, however. The second worst thing is to be told, via form letter, that there are no vacancies for teachers with your qualifications, so you need not apply.

But if you have gotten any sense at all of what sort of need you can fill in the school and have managed to communicate this in person and in your letter, you will probably be invited to submit your resume, either to the person you spoke to or to someone else, perhaps in the board of education's personnel office. Alternatively, you may be asked to fill out an application form.

Don't put off sending in this information. You have their attention now. Don't let it wander.

If you send the information to someone other than the person you spoke to, mention that s/he suggested you submit it. This often helps get your application processed as quickly as possible. But, if you can, avoid the personnel office. You'll lose most of the advantage you gained through your hard work and preparation.

Now you must fight the urge to call up every afternoon and shout into the phone, "Well? Did I get the job? Huh? Did I?" It's tacky. You just have to wait and let the wheels of the public education employment system roll along on their slow course.

In many school districts, the school board gives final approval to all hiring. This is often a kind of rubber stamp approval, and the principal is the one who really does the choosing. But it takes time, all the same.

If they (the school board, personnel office, or whatever) like you, they'll probably ask you to come in for an interview, or possibly several interviews. Remember your conversation with the principal (or whoever it was you asked for "advice"), and you'll do fine. Also remember that you're perfect for this job—because its qualifications are perfect for you.

If All Else Fails

Nothing is fail-safe, especially where finding a job is concerned. If you don't get a specific job, you'll have a pretty good idea why. Either you're not sufficiently qualified for the job you want, or the schools you wanted to work for would like to hire you but can't afford any more staff, or the job just doesn't exist. You'll have to make some adjustments to your expectations. Given the current state of teacher employment in the United States, you'll probably be sent back to the drawing board at least once.

But the effort you've expended hasn't been wasted. You will have gotten an education in how a number of schools are run (or aren't run, in some cases). You will have gotten loads of free advice from people who know what they are talking about. You will have learned a little more about what you want to do with your life. So you must use what you have learned. Maybe you should get a little more education, or consider working in a different area of the country.

If all else fails, you can still send out hundreds of resumes to school districts all over the country.

Your Resume

Most people write a resume completely wrong. They include a great amount of information that is absolutely useless to the person reading the resume. No matter how experienced you are and how many great things you've done, if your *vita* runs over two pages, the remainder won't get read.

Certain things must be included. You must indicate what kind of teaching certification you have. If you're applying for a job in another state, it may be a good idea to list briefly what your certification means—what its requirements are and what you're certified to do. Describe your student teaching assignment.

List your degrees and additional courses you've taken to broaden your knowledge of your field. Your educational background is a very important gauge of your suitability for a job. Be complete. But be concise.

Give your complete employment history, as briefly as possible. Stress any teaching or other work experience with the particular age group you want to teach. If you don't have much work experience to speak of, list what you've done as a volunteer or in a school organization that could apply to your job as a teacher. Don't go overboard on this, though. Personnel officers are particularly good at seeing through a snow job, and too much filler will make them think you're trying to put something over on them. And that's not good public relations.

The idea is to come across as a professional. Be factual, straightforward, and complete. Above all, don't leave any gaps in your employment record. Any unaccounted period over a few months raises doubts about your honest presentation of yourself. It's much better to have "unemployed" on your resume than to make a personnel officer wonder what you have to hide. Being out of work is no shame. At any one time, five to eight percent of all Americans are out of work. (If you prefer the sound of the phrase "laid off," by all means use that.)

Be neat. Nothing strikes a resume reader quite so adversely as a person who's trying to make a good impression through a messy resume. If this is the best you can do, imagine the worst!

Use action words. If you led a scout group, don't say, "Was leader of..." Say, "Led..." You did it—it wasn't done to you. And it is surprising how much more interesting and positive a resume sounds when you get rid of all those passive phrases.

Long Distance

What if you want a job in a distant town—one where you can't just run over during lunch hour to talk to a few people? How do you do your research then? You will have to do most of it long distance, by phone or letter. There are several organizations that can be good sources of information.

First of all, get in touch with the local teachers' union. They know firsthand exactly what the employment situation is at any particular school. And if you get a particularly talkative person on the phone (or a long letter-writer), you'll be able to get all kinds of information: names of teachers at the school, approximate student population, rumors about school mergers and staff cuts, and maybe even the name of the person you will want to speak to about working there.

If there's no union local, write to the state headquarters. Ask for the name of a local teacher you can contact to find out more about working in the town in question. Find out if the union has ever tried to organize the local schools; if not, why not? The reason may convince you that it's either a bad place to work or it's a good place.

Write to the local and state Chambers of Commerce. This organization can give you all kinds of information about a town, from the names of the school principals on down to the average yearly rainfall. Part of what they do is encourage people to come to their town, so they are usually more than happy to answer your questions.

Go to your library. If the town is in the same state, there's a chance your library may have its local paper on file. If so, you've struck it rich. You'll know all the town's gossip, from city hall on down. The smaller the town, the more newspaper space is devoted to the schools.

If you can't get the papers at your library, consider writing to the paper for a long-distance subscription. You'll have to pay for postage, but you'll make up for it in knowledge of the town.

Other things at your library: Census information, broken down by age, sex, economic level, number of persons in a household, and other categories. Regional business directories, which can tell you the economic base of the town. (If it's a company town, that's something you should know before you start to work there.) Names of local colleges and universities (to see who you'll be competing with).

Researching long distance like this can get you only so far. You'll have to plan to visit each place you're interested in, if it's at all possible. And try to visit more than once. It's going to take more than one day to find out all about your possible new home. When you visit, try to have your day planned out in advance. If you've made appointments to talk to a few teachers and other school personnel, you'll get a lot of information in a short time. Don't neglect to take a short tour of the town. Is it the kind of place you would like to live and work? Look around the school district, too, to see the neighborhoods of the kids you'll be teaching.

Research done, you should proceed much as if you were working from close at hand. Play it the same way. Talk to the same level of person, act the same self-respecting, professional you.

Your School Placement Office

We have purposely left this till later, because we wanted you to realize that *you* are responsible for your own career happiness. Nobody else can choose a job for you that will satisfy you as much as the one you choose for yourself. That said, we must now tell you that your college's placement office can give you quite a bit of help in your job search. Depending on the size of your school, there may be a wealth of job listings on file in the office.

It's a strange fact that some jobs can remain open for very long periods, even in a profession where competition is so keen as in teaching. This is true for even the most desirable assignments. For some reason, the correct applicant and job qualifications just haven't met yet. But it's a tremendous oversight for you to neglect the job file just because "there aren't any good jobs left if everybody knows about them."

If your school has an active placement office, schools may come to them in search of qualified job candidates. You can keep your resume on file in the office, to be inspected by any hiring officer who comes along looking for teachers.

This is a very valuable service. In effect, you are making contact with schools who need teachers, without any effort on your part. The only thing you must do is to keep your resume up-to-date, with all your job experience shown and with your current address. This resume may be kept on file even after you are hired by a school, and it may continue to bring you job offers.

Another service often provided by placement offices is to help you decide where and in what kind of school you want to teach. In other words, they help you answer the questions about yourself listed in the beginning of this chapter. You may be given a test or interviewed by a placement officer to determine your interests and skills.

I recommend this service with certain qualifiers. If you use it to help facilitate your getting the answers to the basic questions about your goals and needs, it's good. If you use it to avoid independently thinking about these questions, by looking to the interviewer or the test to answer them for you, it's very bad. By graduation time you have reached a crucial point in your life. You will no longer be sheltered in the arms of school; you will have to go out and do it on your own. And any part of your life decisions you leave to others is a part of your growth process you've thrown away.

Don't waste any time, but take your time. You can afford to be methodical and careful.

Placement Agencies

Since the early 1970's, when teachers began to have trouble finding jobs, many teacher placement agencies have sprung up. They promise to match your qualifications to a list of jobs they just happen to have handy.

Their services range from good to terrible. And it's difficult to judge which kind of agency you've got until you work with them for a while. If you do want to use an agency, your best bet is to interview *them* before they interview you. How many teachers have they placed in the last year? Out of how many applicants? What are the terms of the placement contract? Contracts often specify that you pay a certain percentage of your first year's salary when you've accepted a job offer through them.

Ask for references—people they've found jobs for. And get more than one name. Follow up. Ask how much time the employment counselor spent with them. How long they had to wait for a job offer. How many unsuitable jobs they were offered before they took the one they now have.

Agencies may be beneficial if you are looking for a job in a distant city. You have fewer resources than they do to check on job possibilities. But check their references.

13 OTHER OPPORTUNITIES FOR TEACHERS

Public or private school is not the only employment choice for those who want to be teachers or to work in education. There is a whole range of other opportunities.

Jobs in Private Industry

Banks, large corporations, technical products, and many other companies use teachers to train and provide orientation for their employees. Some multinational corporations employ teachers of languages to prepare their personnel who are being transferred to other countries.

Textbook and learning materials firms employ "demonstration teachers" to show how their products are used. These demonstrations may take place at trade shows, special school board meetings, or professional conventions. The job often combines the two skills of teaching and salesmanship.

Textbook publishers often employ teachers or those with educational training to edit or write texts. Very specialized knowledge is usually required, both of the educational subject of the text and of the publishing process. In fact, teachers are often the only people qualified to do this work.

Teachers also are employed by companies that design and manufacture educational materials, such as filmstrips or learning kits. These jobs usually require a very specific educational background, in early childhood education, for example, with an emphasis in learning materials (yes, courses *are* taught on that subject).

Local and state councils on higher education may offer employment opportunities, perhaps as a liaison with a local school board, a coordinator for special projects, or in public relations.

Research firms use a teacher's talents for evaluating products, doing market studies, or conducting opinion research. If you have the proper training, you may even be hired to work on

*Former teachers may work in a wide variety of other jobs, such as in
the book publishing industry.*

designing the studies. Your talents also might be useful to a variety of publications as a background researcher or writer.

Union offices, such as the American Federation of Teachers, and professional organizations, such as the National Education Association, often employ former teachers as public relations officers, researchers, complaint investigators, organizers, and the like. State and national associations of junior colleges, colleges, and universities may have similar jobs for a limited number of candidates.

Daycare centers are springing up all over the country. This is an excellent, if not well-paid, opportunity for teachers of young children. Depending on the licensing requirements in your locality, you might also be able to open your own daycare center.

A few teachers also get the chance to teach on television. Many states have an educational television station that broadcasts programs used in the schools. The best opportunities are available for those trained to teach a specific subject, even if the program is geared to the elementary grades.

Federal and State Jobs for Teachers

The federal government, through the Defense Department, employs about 7,000 teachers overseas in the DOD Dependent Schools. These schools are operated for the children of U.S. military personnel. The bases are scattered in the four corners of the world, and you may be able to find happiness teaching under a tropical sun or on top of the Alps. Not too many jobs are available—apparently many of the DOD teachers are career civil servants—and the employment conditions in some countries are primitive, but it is a great way to see the world. If you're interested, contact the DOD Dependent Schools and ask for an application and the latest announcement of opportunities.

DOD Dependent Schools
2461 Eisenhower Avenue
Alexandria, VA 22331

The State Department also has a network of schools for dependents of its employees. They often are attached to an embassy in a foreign capital. To find out more about opportunities in these schools, write to:

U.S. Department of State
Office of Overseas Schools
Washington, DC 20525

There are also American-style schools, which are privately supported, in various countries. The requirements for teaching in these schools are much the same as in the States.

Some of these schools often post open positions in college placement offices. Others advertise in the professional journals. You may be able to find out more information about individual schools by writing to the State Department. A list of member schools is available from the European Council of International Schools.

ECIS, Inc.
19 Claremont Rd.
Surbiton, Surrey Kt6 4 QR
England

Other opportunities at home or abroad provided by the federal government come under Action, the umbrella recruiting group for VISTA and the Peace Corps, as well as for a few other groups.

VISTA stands for Volunteers In Service To America. They need teachers and social workers for the poorest and most deprived areas of our country. The pay is minimal, but the rewards may be great if you are interested in serving your fellow human beings.

The same goes for the Peace Corps, except that it operates in small villages in foreign countries. It can also be a real adventure, for those with such leanings.

Contact Action at the address below, and state whether you want to work in the U.S. or abroad. Requirements are somewhat looser for these jobs than for many others in teaching.

Action
26 Federal Plaza
New York, NY 10007

Overseas Opportunities, Part 2

If you would like to work in a specific foreign country as a teacher, you can find out about that country's teacher needs by writing to the Secretary of Public Instruction at the national capital or at the country's embassy office. Your local reference librarian can help find the address. If the country you're interested in is in Central or South America, you can contact its officials through the:

Pan American Union
Washington, DC 20006

Abroad at Home

Finally, there are the U.S. Indian Schools, administered by the Bureau of Indian Affairs of the U.S. Department of the Interior. "Anglo" teachers who want to teach Indians must be able to accept the cultural identity of Indian children and not try to "Americanize" them. After all, they have first call on that word.

Teachers for the Indian Schools are appointed by the Area Director for particular U.S. districts. Decisions are made on the basis of the Civil Service Examination.

Opportunities in American Possessions and Territories

Contact the following offices to find out about opportunities and certification requirements.

Virgin Islands

Commissioner of Education
Government of the Virgin Islands
Charlotte Amalie
P.O. Box 630
St. Thomas, VI 00801

American Samoa

Director of Manpower Resources
Government of American Samoa
Pago Pago, Tutuila, American Samoa 96920

Trust Territory of the Pacific Islands

Recruitment Officer
Trust Territory of the Pacific Islands
Building S-112
Fort Mason
San Francisco, CA 94123

Guam

Assistant Superintendent for Personnel
Department of Education
Government of Guam
P.O. Box D.E.
Agana, GU 96910

APPENDIX
CERTIFICATION REQUIREMENTS

State certification requirements are by no means consistent, and the requirements are phrased in slightly different terms.

Many states have what is known as *reciprocity agreements.* They agree to recognize teacher certification granted under another state's requirements. You can find out if one state's certification is valid in another by writing to that state's board of education in the capital. Find out the address from your reference librarian.

The following listing uses these abbreviations: BA and MA stand for the bachelor's and master's degree, respectively. Different states may call them by different names. Requirements for additional course work beyond the degree are noted as a number, representing semester hours of graduate work. *Renewable* means the certification is renewable for a certain period; *nonrenewable* means it is not and you must get the higher certification to continue teaching; *permanent* means just that.

Alabama
Teacher
   Basic: BA (renewable)
   Intermediate: MA (renewable)
   Professional: MA + 30 (renewable)
Principal
   Basic: MA
   Intermediate: MA + 30
Counselor
   Basic: MA
   Intermediate: MA + 30
Special Education
   Basic: MA
   Intermediate: MA
   Professional: MA + 30

Arkansas

Teacher
  Professional: BA (renewable)
Principal
  Professional: MA
Counselor
  Professional: MA
Special Education
  Professional: MA

California

Teacher
  Basic: BA (nonrenewable)
  Professional: MA
Principal
  Professional: BA + unspecified training
Counselor
  Basic: BA (nonrenewable)
  Professional: BA + 30
Special Education
  Professional: BA + unspecified training

Colorado

Teacher
  Basic: BA
  Professional: MA
Principal
  Professional: MA + 15 or 30 (renewable)
Counselor
  Professional: MA + 30
Special Education
  Professional: MA

Connecticut

Teacher
  Basic: BA
  Professional: BA + 30
Principal
  Basic: MA
  Professional: MA + 30
Counselor
  Basic: MA + 30
  Professional: MA + 45
Special Education
  Basic: BA
  Professional: BA + 30

Delaware

Teacher
  Professional: BA
Principal
  Professional: MA
Counselor
  Professional: MA

District of Columbia

Teacher
  Professional: BA
Principal
  Not specified
Counselor
  Professional: MA
Special Education
  Professional: BA

Florida

Teacher
  Professional: BA or higher (renewable)

Principal
   Professional: MA
Counselor
   Professional: MA or BA + 21

Georgia

Teacher
   Basic: BA
   Professional: MA
Principal
   Professional: MA
Counselor
   Professional: MA
Special Education
   Professional: MA

Hawaii

Teacher
   Basic: BA
   Professional: BA + 30 (renewable)
Principal
   Professional: MA or BA + 30
Counselor
   Basic: BA
   Professional: BA + 30
Special Education
   Basic: BA
   Professional: BA + 30

Idaho

Teacher
   Basic: BA
   Professional: MA

Principal
    Professional: MA
Counselor
    Professional: MA
Special Education
    Basic: BA
    Professional: MA or BA + 30

Illinois

Teacher
    Professional: BA
Principal
    Professional: MA
Counselor
    Professional: MA
Special Education
    Professional: BA

Indiana

Teacher
    Basic: BA (renewable once)
    Professional: MA
Principal
    Basic: MA
    Professional: MA + 15
Counselor
    Basic: MA
    Professional: MA + 18

Iowa

Teacher
    Basic: BA
    Professional: MA
Principal
    Professional: MA + 30

Counselor
  Professional: MA
Special Education
  Basic: BA
  Professional: MA

Kansas

Teacher
  Professional: BA (renewable)
Principal
  Professional: MA (or higher)
Counselor
  Professional: MA

Kentucky

Teacher
  Basic: BA
  Professional: MA
Principal
  Professional: MA
Counselor
  Basic: MA
  Professional: MA + 30
Special Education
  Basic: BA, lifetime with BA + 30 and experience
  Professional: MA

Louisiana

Teacher
  Professional: BA
Principal
  Professional: MA
Counselor
  Professional: MA
Special Education
  Professional: BA

Maine

Teacher
  Basic: BA (renewable)
  Professional: BA + 30 (renewable)
Principal
  Basic: BA + 6
  Professional: MA
Counselor
  Not specified

Maryland

Teacher
  Basic: BA
  Professional: MA or BA + 15
Principal
  Professional: MA
Counselor
  Professional: MA or BA + 30

Massachusetts

Teacher
  Professional: BA or higher
Principal
  Professional: BA or higher
Counselor
  Professional: BA or MA
Special Education
  Professional: BA

Michigan

Teacher
  Basic: BA
  Professional: BA + 18

Principal
   No special certificate; must hold teacher's
Counselor
   Professional: BA

Minnesota

Teacher
   Professional: BA
Principal
   Professional: MA + 30 (or specialist or higher)
Counselor
   Professional: BA + 30 or MA

Mississippi

Teacher
   Basic I: BA
   Basic II: MA
   Intermediate: Specialist or MA + 45
   Professional: Ph.D. or Ed.D
Principal
   Basic: BA + 12
   Intermediate: MA
Counselor
   Basic I: BA + 18
   Basic II: MA
   Intermediate: MA + experience
   Professional: Ph.D. or Ed.D.

Missouri

Teacher
   Professional: BA
Principal
   Professional: MA
Counselor
   Professional: MA

Montana

Teacher
  Basic: BA (education degree in progress)
  Intermediate: BA (ed)
  Professional: BA + 30
Principal
  Basic: MA
  Professional: nonspecified
Counselor
  Professional: BA

Nebraska

Teacher
  Basic: BA
  Intermediate: BA + experience
  Professional: MA or BA + 45
Principal
  Basic: MA or 6-year program
  Professional: 6-year program + recommendation
Counselor
  Not specified

Nevada

Teacher
  Basic: BA
  Professional: MA
Principal
  Professional: MA
Counselor
  Basic: BA
  Professional: MA

New Hampshire

Teacher
  Basic: BA
  Professional: BA + experience

Principal
    Professional: MA
Counselor
    Unspecified graduate work

New Jersey

Teacher
    Professional: BA
Principal
    Professional: MA
Counselor
    Professional: BA or higher

New Mexico

Teacher
    Basic: BA (renewable once)
    Professional: unspecified
Principal
    Basic: MA
    Professional: MA + 30
Counselor
    Basic: BA
    Professional: MA

New York

Teacher
    Basic: BA (nonrenewable)
    Professional: MA
Principal
    Basic: BA + 30 (nonrenewable)
    Professional: MA
Counselor
    Basic: BA + 30
    Professional: MA

North Carolina

Teacher
  Basic: BA
  Professional: MA
Principal
  Basic: MA
  Professional: MA + 30
Counselor
  Professional: MA (or sixth-year program)

North Dakota

Teacher
  Professional: BA (renewable)
Principal
  Professional: MA
Counselor
  Basic: BA
  Professional: MA
Special Education
  Basic: BA
  Intermediate: BA + 6
  Professional: MA or Ph.D.

Ohio

Teacher
  Basic: BA
  Intermediate: BA + 18 + current employment
  Professional: MA or BA + 30
Principal
  Basic: MA
  Intermediate: MA + 15
  Professional: above + 45 months' experience
Counselor
  Basic: MA
  Intermediate: MA + 15
  Professional: above + 45 months' experience

Oklahoma

Teacher
   Basic: BA
   Professional: BA + 32
Principal
   Professional: MA
Counselor
   Basic: MA
   Professional: MA + 32
Special Education
   Professional: BA

Oregon

Teacher
   Basic: BA
   Professional: MA
Principal
   Basic: MA
   Professional: MA + 22
Counselor
   Basic: BA + 18
   Professional: BA + 36

Pennsylvania

Teacher
   Basic: BA
   Professional: BA + 24
Principal
   Basic: Nonspecified Graduate program
   Professional: Three years's experience with above
Counselor
   Basic: BA
   Professional: BA + 24

Rhode Island

Teacher
  Basic: BA (nonrenewable)
  Professional: BA + 36 or MA
Principal
  Basic: MA or BA + 36
  Professional: Above + 15
Counselor
  Basic: BA
  Professional: MA or BA + 36

South Carolina

Teacher
  Professional: BA
Principal
  Professional: MA
Counselor
  Professional: BA + 18

South Dakota

Teacher
  Professional: BA
Principal
  Professional: MA
Counselor
  Professional: MA or BA + 24

Tennessee

Teacher
  Professional: BA
Principal
  Professional: MA
Counselor
  Professional: BA + 38

Texas

Teacher
  Basic: BA
  Professional: BA + 30
Principal and Counselor not specified

Utah

Teacher
  Basic: BA
  Professional: BA + 36 or MA
Principal
  Basic: BA + experience (renewable twice)
  Professional: BA + 2-year graduate program
Counselor
  Basic: MA or BA + 36
  Professional: Above + experience

Vermont

Teacher
  Basic: BA
  Professional: MA or BA + 30
Principal
  Professional: BA + 24
Counselor
  Professional: BA
Special Education
  Professional: BA

Virginia

Teacher
  Professional: BA
Principal
  Professional: nonspecified graduate education

Counselor
    Professional: MA
Special Education
    Professional: BA

Washington

Teacher
    Basic: BA + 30
    Intermediate and Professional: by recommendation
Principal
    Basic: BA + 36
    Professional: MA
Counselor
    Not specified

West Virginia

Teacher
    Basic: BA
    Intermediate: BA + 30
    Professional: MA
Principal
    Basic: MA
    Intermediate: MA + experience
Counselor
    Basic: MA
    Professional: MA + experience
Special Education
    Basic: BA
    Professional: MA

Wisconsin

Teacher
    Professional: BA
Principal
    Professional: BA + nonspecified graduate program

Counselor
    Basic: BA
    Professional: MA or BA + 30

Wyoming

Teacher
    Basic: BA
    Intermediate: BA + experience
    Professional: MA
Principal
    Basic: MA
    Intermediate: MA + 15
    Professional: above + experience
Counselor
    Basic: BA
    Intermediate: MA
    Professional: MA + 30

INDEX